Learning with AI

Learning with AI

THE K–12 TEACHER'S GUIDE TO A NEW ERA OF HUMAN LEARNING

Joan Monahan Watson

with José Antonio Bowen and C. Edward Watson

JOHNS HOPKINS UNIVERSITY PRESS
Baltimore

© 2024 Johns Hopkins University Press
All rights reserved. Published 2024
Printed in the United States of America on acid-free paper
2 4 6 8 9 7 5 3 1

Johns Hopkins University Press
2715 North Charles Street
Baltimore, Maryland 21218
www.press.jhu.edu

Library of Congress Cataloging-in-Publication Data is available.
A catalog record for this book is available from the British Library.

ISBN: 978-1-4214-5120-6 (paperback)
ISBN: 978-1-4214-5121-3 (ebook)

Special discounts are available for bulk purchases of this book. For more information,
please contact Special Sales at specialsales@jh.edu.

CONTENTS

CHRONOLOGY

1950s Artificial intelligence research gets going but is focused on expert or logical systems.

1959 Arthur Samuel coins the term "machine learning"

1967 Joseph Weizenbaum creates Eliza, the first significant chatbot and LLM, which marked the beginning of work into natural language processing (NLP).

1980s Faster and cheaper hardware helps stir a revival in machine learning as an AI strategy.

1990s Deep Learning and Artificial Neural Network research begins to grow.

1997 IBM's DeepBlue beats Garry Kasparov in chess.

2010 DeepMind founded by Demis Hassabis, Shane Legg, and Mustafa Suleyman.

2014 Ian Goodfellow proposes Generative Adversarial Networks, which lead to many new types of neural networks that are both generative and able to be trained.

2016 AlphaGo (a machine-learning AI from DeepMind) beats world champion Lee Sedol at Go.

2017 Transformers make it possible to both decode and generate new text.

2018 First GPT LLM created by OpenAI.

2021 DALL-E, built on GPT 3, is a machine-learning model that generates images.

2022 GPT 3.5 launched in November; AI apps begin to proliferate.

2023 GPT 4 released in March, followed by Bard (by Google), Claude (by Anthropic), LLaMA (by Meta) and Grok (by X).

2024 ChatGPT 4o leads the way in May as LLMs get smaller, faster, multimodal (able to see and hear), emotionally sensitive, and more integrated with the release of Apple Intelligence.

Learning with AI

Introduction

Nothing in life is to be feared, it is only to be understood.
Now is the time to understand more, so that we may fear less.

MARIE CURIE, Nobel Laureate in Physics (1903)
and Chemistry (1911)

Understanding what AI is and how it works poses vast challenges. Like the internet, AI is a technology that is going to change everything—and not just education.

The internet, and more specifically, the World Wide Web, fundamentally changed our relationship with knowledge, moving us from a world in which knowledge was scarce (but mostly reliable) to one in which knowledge is abundant (but largely unreliable). When this framing was first floated (Bowen, 2006), we were all using the internet on our desktops: the iPhone was yet to arrive. We could all appreciate the increased access to research materials and expertise, but we were already wary of the rise of unfiltered and sometimes sinister misinformation. And with the struggles of dial-up, it was easy to underestimate the coming ubiquity of the new technology. Speed, ease of access, and platforms changed the mechanics and magnified the effect but not the trajectory. Our relationship with knowledge changed forever, and in turn everything from education and shopping to culture and politics changed as well.

Just as the internet changed our relationship with knowledge, AI is going to change our relationship with thinking. It's already challenging ideas about creativity and originality, and it will forever alter education, work, and even how we think about thinking (both human and AI "thinking").

Perhaps we can learn some lessons from the rise of the internet. Just as later technologies (like the iPhone and social media) amplified the effects of the internet, we can assume that AI is going to improve and grow more intertwined with our lives. Banning students' use of web-based tools like Wikipedia failed, but would the internet have turned out differently if we had put different constraints on how it developed?

AI has already challenged and divided us faster than the internet did. Some of what we present will have evolved by the time this book is published. Still, in 2006, we didn't need to understand the specific convergence devices or social media platforms that were to come in order to know that information would soon be less reliable. Rapid change is again unfolding, and we can use what AI can already do to plan for a future in which our relationship with thinking will be fundamentally altered.

Ethics and Equity

We have tried to keep this book short and focused on the practical. On almost every page, we could have delved deeper into ethical problems and ambiguities. Someone else will write that book.

As we learned from the internet and social media, there are a million ways that the expansion of AI could go wrong and increase inequities, take jobs, and damage human lives. But if you watch Netflix, use a spam filter, shop at Amazon, or drive a car, you are already a part of the new AI economy. The creation of consumer-grade, more human-sounding chatbots has brought attention to AI and is a breakthrough that will change our lives. The implications of being able to process virtually anything (data, music, images, computer code, DNA, or brain waves) as language and at scale, however, is mind-blowing and needs careful consideration. As much as many of us would like to, this is not the time to put our heads in the sand until this whole AI thing blows over. Even if we choose to ignore it, AI is not going away—and it's only getting more sophisticated with each passing moment. Teachers of students in compulsory K–12 education in the United States have an often unspecified and unwritten but highly enforced social contract. As we prepare students to become global citizens, it's our responsibility to help them develop into thoughtful, responsible, and ethical adults. To that end, and given the ubiquity of AI, we need to explore meaningful opportunities to integrate AI literacy across our K–12 curriculum.

AI is already increasing inequity both in education and beyond, but it also has the potential to be a tool for equity: AI can provide more feedback to improve learning, increase human creativity, and customize materials for groups or individual students. Teachers will be in an important position to determine whether AI transforms education for better or worse. In the chapters that follow, we have tried to provide multiple examples of the transformational power of AI with the goal of offering the most practical and urgent information.

You won't like every suggestion or application of AI, but we avoided too much commentary to keep the book from becoming a brick. We have left space for you to make up your own mind.

Students

We quote as much data on how students are using AI as we could find, but given the speed at which things are changing, we also did our own research. We talked to a lot of students, mostly in small groups. We interviewed students from different grades and different backgrounds. To protect their privacy, we do not identify these students, nor do we quote them directly, but the information they shared was highly instructive and occasionally shocking. Their personal stories (and frank admissions) add context and a sense of grounding as we move through the chapters that follow.

Your students may be different, but we urge you to consider that students don't like admitting to their teachers (or to their parents or to researchers, for that matter) that they've cheated or engaged in what might be viewed as questionable or embarrassing practices. In the same way that voters often say one thing in a survey and then do another at the ballot box, the students we interviewed consistently reported that almost everyone in their orbit was using AI. Even early elementary school students had been exposed to AI through older siblings, who helped them write stories, or through their parents, who helped them create special coloring sheets. A small group of middle school kids told us that there is no way that they're ever going to use AI. When we asked why, one student said it was because AI is "super-scary, and it will probably take my mom's job." Later that day, in a different context, that same student was overheard asking Siri to "find the words to that Taylor Swift song that starts 'You take a deep breath/And you walk through the doors . . .'" Scared of AI, indeed!

Many of the high school students we spoke to were quick to point out that there were lots of different ways to use AI and that they did not consider many of of these to be cheating. This is certainly a valid point that we address throughout this book. That said—and in a moment of sheer heartbreak—one cheeky junior laughed and said that AI would make it easier for his mom to write his papers. Sigh.

Organization

This book is divided into three parts: A Brave New Context, Teaching with AI, and Learning with AI.

Part I examines how AI works and what it is doing to the human experience. Chapter 1 starts with terms and enough history to illuminate why the advent of AI seems so sudden. It's a far more technical chapter than what you will find the remainder of the book, but for those of you who want to understand the magic behind the curtain, it'll give you a glimpse.

Chapter 2 chronicles the appearance of AI in "the wild"—beyond its use in education—and how the world of work (and even job interviews) is being impacted. That fearful middle schooler isn't wrong: AI will eliminate some jobs, and it will probably change how each of us works. This could be good or bad, but we are all likely to be asked to do more work better and more quickly. (And as teachers, we are no strangers to such requests.)

AI literacy requires knowing enough about how AI works to be able to use it effectively. Breaking down problems and asking better questions have long been a cornerstone of teaching and learning, and these are critical skills in using AI. Chapter 3 explores a general definition of AI Literacy and divides this process into categories—from articulating the problem, finding the right AI for the task, creating better prompts, and then iterating with AI. Emphasizing the importance of professional development for teachers and addressing critical issues presented by the use of AI in schools such as safety, privacy, and ethical use, chapter 4 outlines strategies for introducing AI to students at different grade levels, from using AI as a "class pet" in elementary schools to teaching critical thinking and prompt engineering in high school, while also highlighting the need to be aware of AI's potential for hallucinations and bias.

Part II shifts the focus to teaching and how the benefits that come from AI are rooted in our own professional knowledge, thinking, and expertise. Chapter 5 explores ways in which AI may function as a reliable assistant for completing administrative tasks that overfill our plates and lead to burnout, while chapter 6 focuses on the uniquely creative nature of AI: As a prediction machine without the inhibitions of social embarrassment, AI will "say" anything. The problem of "hallucinating" becomes a strength when the task is coming up with new ideas. It's in this chapter and in chapter 7 that we introduce AI as a creative assistant who is able to generate fun, exciting lesson plans and teaching materials that are aligned with standards and learning outcomes—and that will also provide adaptive planning for classroom individualized education programs (IEPs) and other specialized instructional needs. We conclude this second part with chapter 8, which offers guidance on establishing and integrating AI policies and practices through the expansion and further promotion of existing "digital citizenship" standards as we transition to discussions of students "behind the wheel" with AI.

Our focus for part III is on designing assessments and assignments that position AI as a learning assistant for students. In chapter 9 we explore assignment redesigns that place greater value on human effort, make cheating far less rewarding and useful, and ultimately engage students in more cognitively significant learning tasks. If students are collaborating with AI to produce better work, they're clearly onto something. What we call cheating, businesses see as innovation in this new AI era.

Chapter 10 considers how AI can customize learning and create individual feedback for students. Chapter 11 outlines new design principles and how we can better guide learning processes to make them visible. Chapter 12 applies these principles through numerous examples, and outlines how teachers can experiment with new ideas to support learning with AI.

Prompts and Responses

We obviously spent a lot of time testing ideas with different AIs. We list many of our specific prompts identified with a gray bar on the left. We wanted it to be very clear when we were quoting directly from an AI, so we've listed AI responses in italics, with a gray bar on the right. We've also listed the AI we used, the version, and the date (Style manuals currently only suggests the date, but the version—GPT 3.5, 4, or 4o, for example—also matters.) AIs tend to be verbose, so most of the responses are abridged (which is also indicated).

We reran prompts as close to the publication date as possible, often with newer versions of a particular AI. Sometimes we left an earlier response or used the old GPT 3.5 response to show what a cheap and basic response might be. Sometimes good is good enough, and we realize that many students and faculty will be limited to free versions. Since prompts will return a different and unique answer each time, we have included responses only when they were important to the point at hand: showing complete responses from multiple AIs would have made this book much longer for limited gain. You'll want to customize and experiment with the prompts yourself.

A Brave New Context

CHAPTER 1

AI Basics

AI is one of the most important things humanity is working on.
It is more profound than electricity or fire.

SUNDAR PICHAI, CEO of Google and Alphabet

If you were busy on November 30, 2022, you might have missed OpenAI's early demo of its new chatbot. But after five days, more than a million people had tried it. It reached 100 million daily active users in two months. It took TikTok nine months and Instagram two and a half years to reach that milestone (Hu, 2023).

But bigger than fire? Sundar Pichai has made this comparison repeatedly, but few of us were listening when he said it publicly in January 2016 while also admitting that he didn't really know how AI worked. Fire, like other human technological achievements, has been a double-edged sword: a source of destruction and change as well as an accelerant to beneficial advancements. AI is already on a similar trajectory.

Most of us have heard of AI; some may even remember when a computer beat the chess world champion, but that was a different sort of AI. As happens in many fields (think mRNA vaccines), research over decades takes a turn or finds a new application, and a technology that has been evolving over years suddenly bursts into public awareness.

For centuries, humans looked for easy ways to rekindle fire in the middle of the night. Early chemical versions from Robert Boyle (in the 1680s) to Jean Chancel (1805) were expensive, dangerous, or both, and none made it to mass production. Then, in 1826, chemist John Walker accidentally discovered that friction could make the task of starting a fire safe and cheap. Like matches, seventy years of scholarly work in AI helped create the recent explosion of awareness, but in a flicker, our world has changed.

Expert Systems vs. Machine Learning

The term **artificial intelligence** (AI) was coined in 1956 at a conference sponsored by the Defense Advanced Research Projects Agency (DARPA) to imagine, study, and create machines capable of performing tasks that typically require human cognition and intelligence. (We've highlighted key terms when they are first defined and summarized them in the sidebar glossaries.)

Early AI research focused on logic or **expert systems** that used rules designed to anticipate a wide range of possible scenarios. These systems don't improve with more iterations, though robots and AI are often thus portrayed in fiction. Even in *Star Trek*, the emergency medical hologram is constantly limited by its programming.

IBM pioneer Arthur Samuel (1959) coined the term **machine learning** to describe statistical algorithms that could generalize and "learn to play a better game of checkers than can be played by the person who wrote the program." For a simple game like checkers, it was possible to develop an expert system that could search a database but also make inferences beyond existing solutions. Samuel's checkers program, however, was "given only the rules of the game, a sense of direction, and a redundant and incomplete list of parameters which are thought to have something to do with the game, but whose correct signs and relative weights are unknown and unspecified" (Samuel, 1959).

Expert systems (and their logical reasoning) initially dominated research, but machine learning (with its probabilistic reasoning) was more useful in recognizing patterns; it became a more central part of AI research in the 1990s (Langley, 2011). With more memory and larger datasets, statistical algorithms were able to deduce medical diagnoses (WebMD, for example) and eventually led to IBM's Deep Blue chess program beating chess champion Garry Kasparov in 1997.

Machine Learning + Neural Networks = Foundational Models

Neural networks are computing systems modeled like the neural connections in the human brain. Neural networks are a specific type of machine-learning model in which **nodes** (individual computational units) are organized into layers that mirror our understanding of the human brain. In the 1960s and '70s, networks were logical and linear if-then structures (like following directions from your GPS), but they have become more decentralized layers of interconnected nodes (like knowing lots of different ways to get between two points).

Neural networks need to be trained, usually on large datasets. This training can be either "supervised," where the data is labeled so that the model learns the associations between inputs and desired outputs, or "unsupervised," where the input data is unlabeled. Once a supervised model is trained, it can classify new inputs: this is how your spam filter works. Unsupervised machine learning generally requires larger datasets but can then associate or cluster unseen trends and relationships: the more you watch Netflix, the more it discovers connections among the things you actually like (and realizes that the documentary about goldfish that you saved was a mistake).

A third machine-learning paradigm (alongside supervised and unsupervised) is **reinforcement learning (RL)**. Here, neural networks are fed often smaller amounts of unlabeled data but allow the algorithm to interact in an environment in which specific outputs are rewarded: when you click on Facebook ads, you're more likely to see those ads again.

Deep learning (DL) is a related training technique in which "deep" refers to the multiple layers of the network needed to transform data; simpler tasks reside deeper in the network and then combine to inform output layers. In facial recognition, for example, the model needs first to recognize which groups of pixels constitute faces before it can extract features and then finally match features to known faces.

These machine-learning techniques mirror both the advantages and the disadvantages of human learning. London-based DeepMind, now a subsidiary of Google, could have taught its Deep Q-Network to play video games like Pong by programming-in the rules (an expert systems approach). This (like cheating) would have been faster, but by using these much slower trial-and-error techniques, Deep Q-Network could now generalize and, like humans, learn the next Atari game much faster. Since the model was learning directly from data, it could also create a strategy in ways not limited by human assumptions (with implications for both creativity [see chapter 6] and accuracy [see below]). These DeepMind programs took longer to learn for themselves but eventually exceeded human capabilities (Mnih et al., 2015).

Together, deep neural networks and machine-learning techniques allow us to build **foundational models.** Since they are trained on very large and varied datasets, they are general-purpose systems whose broad capabilities are still being discovered: few anticipated that these new models could decode brain scans (fMRI) back into the images that subjects were viewing (Chen, 2022; Takagi & Nishimoto, 2023). Part of what makes new AI technology so different, and potentially dangerous, is that we are still discovering what it can do.

Large Language Models (LLMs) are foundational models that were initially focused on language but also created new ways to analyze DNA, music, computer code, and brain waves. The big six LLMs we have today are GPT (from OpenAI), Gemini (from Google), LLaMA (from Meta), Claude (from Anthropic), Pi (from Inflection), Grok (from xAI). (See fig. 1.1.)

Think of these models as different types of intelligence (like comparing Marie Curie, Maya Angelou, and Cesar Chavez). Their neural networks are different, and they've been trained differently: they're different (metaphorically) in both nature and nurture.

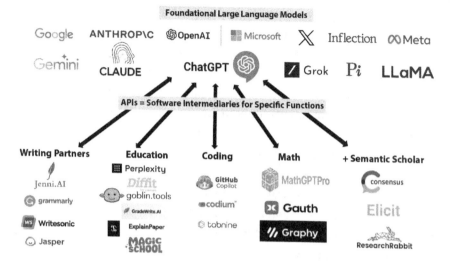

Figure 1.1 The top line shows different Foundational LLMs with some of the software "apps" that interface with them through APIs.

The Turing Test and AI Thinking

Alan Turing first considered the question "Can machines think?" in his paper "Computing Machinery and Intelligence" (Turing, 1950). Turing argued that since "thinking" is hard to define, his original question is meaningless, and he replaced it with a version of the "imitation game" where the interrogator asks two players questions and receives answers, all through text on computer screens. In Turing's twist, one subject is a human and the other is an AI; the interrogator attempts to determine which is the human. What we now call the "Turing Test" is *not* about thinking, consciousness, intelligence, understanding, sentience, or anything to do with *how* a program might be processing; Turing's innovation was replacing the question "Can machines think?" with the question "Can this chatbot make us believe we are interacting with a human?"

In 2022, Google engineer Blake Lemione was fired for claiming that Google's chatbot had become sentient (Grant and Metz, 2022): a clear pass of the Turing Test. An AI does not have to think: *believing* a chatbot is sentient is enough.

LLMs use a combination of technologies to mimic human language and predict the next word, including deep neural networks that mimic human learning, increasing computer speed and capacity, vast amounts of existing human data, and a renewed emphasis on a machine-learning strategy that relies on probability and statistics. In the same way that adding friction to a match creates fire in a new way, the returning focus on probability and machine learning in the 1990s unlocked the door to new generative AI. After encountering GPT-3 in 2020, philosopher David Chalmers wrote "it suggests a potential mindless path to **artificial general intelligence** (or AGI)" (Chalmers, 2020). ChatGPT was a breakthrough, but it was also built on compromises.

Glossary I

Artificial Intelligence (AI) refers to the ability of computer systems to mimic human intelligence and also to the development of such systems.

Expert Systems use rules and logic to anticipate a wide range of possible scenarios.

Machine Learning uses probability and statistics to recognize patterns and generalize.

Neural Networks are computing systems modeled like the neural connections in the human brain.

Foundational Models are deep neural networks trained with a large data set using machine learning techniques that mimic human trial and error.

Large Language Models (LLMs) are foundational models focused on language.

GPT stands for Generative Pre-trained Transformers. Foundational models and LLMs all use GPT architecture; it is not unique to OpenAI or ChatGPT.

Diffusion Models are a type of foundational model used to create images and video. Tools like DALL-E, Stable Diffusion, Midjourney are trained by adding noise to the training data which the model learns to remove.

Hallucinations and Bias: The *G* and the *P* in GPT

The process of pre-training (the *P* in Generative Pre-trained Transformers or GPT models) an AI is lengthy and requires an enormous dataset (GPT-3 was trained on 45 terabytes of textual data: more than 12 trillion words). That is also why Large Language Models are "large." Since the pre-training sources (including the monthly Common Crawl dataset taken from billions of web pages) contain the good, bad, and ugly of human thought, and since LLMs assimilate to predict, they are bound to reproduce the bias and hate in their source material.

AI can also *amplify* the bias on the internet. When Stable Diffusion, an AI capable of creating photorealistic images, is asked to create images related to high-paying jobs, the images are of people (three times more often men than women) with lighter skin tones than when asked about lower-paying jobs. When asked for images of "doctors," only 7% of the images generated are of women, while 39% of doctors in the United States are women: Stable Diffusion exaggerates existing inequities, which is apparent in images in the internet training set (Nicoletti & Bass, 2023). Images generated by other AI image creators also yield biases.

Adobe's Firefly AI image generator tries to correct this by making the number of women or Black doctors proportional to the population of that group in the United States: half the images of doctors it generates are women, and 14% of the doctors are Black, even though only 6% of US doctors are Black (Howard, 2023). Firefly has been trained to increase the probability that a request for an image of a Supreme Court justice in 1960 will be a woman, even though it wasn't until 1981 that Sandra Day O'Connor became the first woman appointed to the court.

Bias can come from training data, but the well-intentioned Firefly examples highlight another set of potential problems: human reviewers who rate and provide feedback for the model's output also have bias. If AIs can create images of the world as it could be or as it is, who gets to choose? Bias can also be hidden in network architecture, decoding algorithms, model goals, and perhaps more worrisome, in the undiscovered potential of these models.

The *G* in GPT stands for "generative." Because these models "generate" new sentences, images, and ideas by sorting probabilities of the next word or pixel, they are prone to "generate" false data or "fabricate" fictional references. This ability to "hallucinate" makes AI a terrific tool for creativity: it will put ideas and words together in ways that humans might never have done before (more on this in chapter 4). This same design feature that allows LLMs to provide new and different answers to the same prompt also causes unpredictability and a lack of reliability. AI can also generate misinformation.

There are ways to reduce both of these problems, but it's difficult to entirely eliminate unpredictability and lack of reliability because both are direct consequences of the ways AIs learn to mimic human thinking. The bias is largely a result of the "Pre-training," and the potential for "hallucination" is built into the "Generative" part of GPT.

Transformers: The *T* in GPT

Understanding the *T* in GPT (transformers, but not the ones you see in movies) is harder and also puts "parameters" and "tokens" in our path.

Every internal variable in a neural network that can be tuned or adjusted to change the output is a **parameter**. A simple parameter is the number of possible words that might go next in a sentence. A hyperparameter is a configuration of variables like the randomness, creativity, or "temperature" of which response is chosen. When the temperature is set to 0, the model is at its most deterministic: it will return the next word with the highest probability. At higher temperatures, less probable words can be chosen, which leads to more creativity and diversity, but also to more potential nonsense and hallucination. The Copilot conversational style buttons—creative, balanced, or precise—seem to regulate temperature. A model is trained by feeding it examples and tuning its parameters to adjust the output.

GPT 2 had 1.5 billion parameters, GPT 3 had 175 billion parameters, and GPT-4 was estimated to have 1.76 trillion parameters and significantly more memory (Griffith, 2023; Geyer, 2023). More parameters allow for more choices and nuance, so GPT 4 is smarter, more factual, more multilingual, and multimodal (able to accept visual or audio prompts). GPT 4 can create graphs, or it can use an image of what is in your refrigerator to generate recipe ideas. But more parameters can also be slower and more costly. For some tasks, GPT 3.5 is good enough or even better, but while GPT 3.5 failed the bar exam, GPT 4 immediately passed, doing better than most humans (Katz et al., 2023). Professor Anna Mills was a beta-tester for GPT 4 and quickly noticed that it wrote more sophisticated, precise, articulate, and connected prose, with more varied sentence structure, word choice, information, and examples than GPT 3.5 (Mills, 2023b). All of those extra parameters allow users to imitate a scholar or to write like Yoda.

A neural network deals only with numbers, so words (or images or brain waves) need to be turned into **tokens,** which are a kind of digital stand-in. Tokens are a series of 0s and 1s that represent words, parts of a word, or other data. More tokens imply more vocabulary, context, and nuance, but both the process of turning words into numbers ("tokenization") and size matter. The largest models now allow you to upload millions of words for analysis at a time. Some models are also multimodal and can tokenize both images and sound.

An AI determines the meaning of a token by observing it in context (i.e., what other tokens—words or images—appear near it and how often). Initially, each word in a sequence was processed sequentially. The 2017 breakthrough of **transformers** (the T you've been waiting for) provided every token with a weight that internalized the context of the token compared with any other token (Uszkoreit, 2017; Vaswani et al., 2017). This "self-attention" allowed each word to be processed simultaneously, which greatly increased speed and created a more "natural" way to embed context. Transformers allow an AI to look not just at the probability of the next token, but also at multiple combinations of tokens and larger patterns at once. Transformers opened the door for human-sounding LLMs but also unified the many disparate disciplines of AI into one of a field where everything—from images, code, music, or DNA—can be treated like language. This synchronicity (which echoes the predictions of a coming convergence or singularity) is one of the reasons why LLMs have become the central foundation models and why change has appeared to occur so quickly. Public access to a functioning GPT on November 30, 2022, also helped shape that perception.

Glossary II

Natural Language Processing (NLP) is a field of AI and linguistics that aims to enable machines to understand, interpret and create human language. They are essential for search engines and analyzing your social media content. LLMs use NLP to train deep neural networks but LLMs are also used in NLP applications.

Parameters are internal variables in a neural network that can be tuned or adjusted to change the output.

Tokens are the representations of words, parts of words, characters, or punctuation in code and are a focus of NLP.

Transformers (or **"self-attention"**) provide every token with a weight that allows tokens to be compared to any other token simultaneously.

An **Application Programming Interface (API)** is a set of tools for building software applications that can interact with a foundation model. Most of the AI tools and products we are using are not LLMs themselves but are powered by underlying LLMs.

Fine-tuning is the process of customizing pre-trained foundational models (using an API) to do specific tasks. There is an ambiguity here, but for most people it is probably close enough to think of ChatGPT as fine-tuned or powered by GPT, and not its own LLM.

Generative Artificial Intelligence (GAI) is any type of AI that uses deep learning models to generate or create new content. LLMs and Diffusion Models are both examples of GAI.

Artificial General Intelligence (AGI) is the computer science holy grail: someday an AI will be able to think, make decisions and even feel like humans can. It's basically a person.

Tools and Trade-offs

The established, publicly accessible LLMs you know all use Generative Pre-trained Transformers (GPT), but they're not all the same:

- Claude seems obsessively focused on safety and making AI obey human values (Rose, 2023). Claude 3.5 and GPT 4 are both rumored to have over 1 trillion parameters, but Claude is built with more tokens. This gives Claude a deeper understanding of context and makes its answers more readable and even poetic and (sometimes) more likely to avoid AI-detection tools (Hines, 2023; Rose, 2023).

- Grok moves in the other direction with fewer safety guardrails and will answer more questions with more humor and sarcasm, although real-time information

from X (formerly Twitter) could be an advantage for
staying current.

- If you used free Chat-GPT from about June 2023
through May 2024, you were using ChatGPT 3.5, which
was not connected to the internet. For specific questions
about something recent, it was likely to create fictional
references. GPT 4 is a substantially smarter and better
AI (as is GPT 4o, for omni); don't assume you understand anything about AI until you've used it for several
hours.

- Microsoft is heavily invested in OpenAI, so Copilot is a
similar, but not identical, experience.

- Apple Intelligence also comes from a partnership with
Open AI and ChatGPT. Apple is aiming to combine
integration and security with your other Apple data by
running a local (and smaller) LLM on your phone that
will keep your data on your phone (but connecting with
ChatGPT when it needs more.)

- Google has its own AI, Gemini, that allows you to click
on highlighted statements or click the "Google button"
that allows you to check the veracity of information
against a web search.

- LLaMA is Meta's family of open-source LLMs, so you can
download an LLM and build your own AI tool. Hugging-
Chat (from Hugging Face) is an application that uses
LLaMA; importantly, it is free with no registration
required.

- Pi is designed to be a conversational personal assistant.
Pi is chatty, but not connected to the internet, so it
works well for practice or learning conversations
(described in chapter 7).

Foundational models can be further fine-tuned for specific tasks. Perplexity is optimized for internet searches, and Poe gives you access to multiple AIs at once. What AI tool you should use depends on what you want to accomplish: Do you want speed, reliability, or clickable links?

New models are now mostly multimodal. The ability to see, speak, and listen means that they can both watch a student work on a math problem with pencil and paper and talk them through the answer.

When the iPhone connected the internet to the phone, we soon realized that we didn't need information about every flight leaving every day; we just needed to know whether our flight today was delayed. An airline app is better for that task. Apps were created to focus on making specific tasks easier and faster. Like the apps on your phone, specialized and often fine-tuned apps using APIs will focus your interaction with base models. Indeed, the new OpenAI store is modeled on the Apple App Store and sells customized "GPTs." You can also fine-tune your own application from the pre-trained LLaMA family.

One group of tools (Elicit, Consensus, and ResearchRabbit) connects ChatGPT with Semantic Scholar's database of 175 million papers to ensure that searches connect you or your students to published research. Most of the educational AIs (from Diffit to Magic School) are really APIs or fine-tuned versions of ChatGPT. With the right data and prompts, you could replicate many of their features, but sometimes a more focused tool is easier and faster.

The top line of figure 1.1 shows the current big six LLMs (from Google, X, OpenAI, Anthropic, Inflection and Meta: expect Apple and Amazon to join). Below them are an array of API tools. Most of these interact with ChatGPT since it was the first to market, but that will change over time. Microsoft and Google are integrating their Copilot and Gemini AIs directly into their other products, and you can add extensions to summarize YouTube videos or plan a vacation on Expedia. The reality is that you won't be able to keep track of all of the AI lurking in your life (and don't even think about what insurance companies, advertisers, or the government could do with the data that your car knows about you), but it will be useful to know about the variety of AIs on the market and which specific tasks each can perform for you (and which does a task better than another).

LearnLM (from Google) and ChatGPT Edu (from Open AI) are both "fine-tuned" to be better conversational tutors for education, and it's clear that the tech giants see education as a potential market. LearnLM is a version of Gemini that has been further trained to encourage active learning, manage cognitive load, deepen metacognition, stimulate curiosity and adapt to learner's needs (Jurenka, Kunesch et al., 2024). Some of this you could do with individual prompts, but you would need to constantly reuse your detailed prompts; this approach also allows the AI to learn and adapt within this pedagogical framework; additional interactions and evaluations from students and teachers helped it do just that. (If prompting is like providing a recipe, fine-tuning is like teaching it to cook.) This approach also circumvents many of the common pitfalls of using a generic AI for tutoring: providing answers, information overload, and agreeing with whatever the learner says.

There are also a growing range of models that are smaller, faster, and cheaper to build and run, like GPT 4o, but also even smaller open-source models like Microsoft Phi-3, Gemma and Apple OpenELM. The trade-offs here are speed and latency: you can talk (and interrupt) an AI running on your phone. These do not have the general intelligence of larger models but can be better at focused and localized tasks, like doing math problems.

Finally, AI "agents" (like Devin) are coming. All of the AIs above are chatbots—they're just talk. AI agents use an application wrapper to allow an LLM to do a series of tasks or multi-step reasoning, acting like an autonomous contractor who can do things like build a website or manage student homework (monitoring when it is completed and creating and then sending individual feedback).

AI is not new: it has been curating your social media feed and recommendations for years. This publicly emerging new wave of AI, however, is different. Previous AI helped *curate* your world (or what you saw and read online), but GPT AI will allow you to *create* your world. We're only beginning to learn what AI can do, but AI literacy will be an essential work- and life-skill for both faculty and students. We need to integrate AI-literacy into our classrooms, but first, we need to understand how it is changing work and the future careers of our students.

CHAPTER 2

AI in the Wild

If we teach today as we taught yesterday,
we rob our children of tomorrow.

JOHN DEWEY

Whether high school graduates choose to enter the workforce or pursue a college degree, they will likely discover a rapidly evolving landscape of thinking, learning, and working. Although most of us have now lived through several major technological changes, generative AI is a different technology, and the way it is changing our lives is different, too.

AI and the Workforce

While previous technological revolutions targeted the skilled but often manual jobs of factory workers, telephone operators, travel agents, and farmers, AI appears set to be more disruptive to lawyers, doctors, copywriters, insurance underwriters, translators, artists, and anyone who works with text. Initial predictions suggest that AI may have little effect in construction (6%

of current work tasks) or building and grounds maintenance (1%) but much larger effects in business and financial operations (35%), science (36%), engineering (37%), legal (44%), and administrative support (46%) (Briggs & Kodnani, 2023). Vast new efficiencies are being discovered across a wide range of white-collar sectors, and the expectation is that the impact will be akin to the industrial revolution: a single individual will accomplish work that previously required a team (Bannon, 2023).

This will be a different type of revolution—not because it eliminates a few categories of work, but because it will change the nature of work for everyone. Jobs are bundles of tasks, so *every* job has some tasks that AI can do better. AI can already produce faster and cheaper patient notes, and it's better at reading scans. That won't eliminate the need for doctors, but it's already changing what doctors do and how they and we think about the most critical skills for doctors in the future. AI will eliminate some jobs altogether, but it's going to change every job: those who can work with AI will replace those who can't.

Previous technology changed the nature of many manual jobs, from sewing by hand to using a sewing machine, from drawing characters to programming animation, and from assembling cars to supervising robots. Generative AI is going to change the way we think, but not just at work. Collaboration with AIs will change the nature of human thinking.

AI Will Change Every Job

Regardless of which jobs high school students assume after graduation, and regardless of how AI ultimately shapes different sectors, AI is going to change every job. The internet was mostly a job creator: while US newsroom jobs (including reporters, editors, and photographers) fell from 114,000 in 2008 to 85,000 in 2020, more than three million people are now employed in IT (Walker, 2021). The internet made research easier; indeed, the number of librarians employed in the United States has not grown since 1990, although total employment has grown by 40%, much of that in computing and programming (Rattner, 2023). Could AI repeat this pattern?

Several new studies consider the impact on jobs. One looked at the 950 job categories listed by the US Department of Labor and concluded that almost every occupation included tasks that would be affected by AI but that few jobs would be completely eliminated (Maslej et al., 2023; Whitten, 2023). A Goldman Sachs report analyzed tasks versus jobs and concluded that two-thirds of current occupations could be partially automated by AI (Briggs & Kodani, 2023).

A similar study found that around 80% of the US workforce could have at least 10% of their work tasks affected by the introduction of the new AIs, while approximately 19% of workers may see at least 50% of their tasks impacted. Fifteen percent of worker tasks could be "completed significantly faster at the same level of quality" with AI (Eloundou et al., 2023). Another study estimates that software engineers using Codex will be twice as productive (Kalliamvakou, 2022), while yet another finds that the ideation, synthesizing, evaluating, writing, coding, data analysis, simulation of human subjects, and mathematical modeling capabilities of AI could make economists 10%–20% more productive (Korinek, 2023).

Another report, published by Amazon Web Services in November 2023, that focused on technology-related skills and jobs found that more than 90% of surveyed employers expect to use AI-related solutions in their organizations by 2028. They also acknowledge that AI-related skills will likely boost pay and career benefits, that workers with AI expertise might see a 35% or more increase in their paychecks, and that, generally speaking, AI could boost productivity for employees and employers alike. What is the most important technology skillset a job candidate can possess, according to the report? AI skills. AI skills outrank application development and the use of cloud-based tools when considering workplace readiness.

As we think about preparing our students for this new era, the good news for teachers is twofold: (1) we can help students acquire these AI skills while they are still with us in the classroom, and (2) critical thinking and problem-solving skills— habits of mind we begin to teach starting in kindergarten—are ranked as even more essential for the effective use of AI than technical skills, such as coding (Amazon Web Services & Access Partnership, 2023). What we're called to do as educators is to provide our students with the literacy and skills they need to navigate their AI-enriched world. According to findings from a student poll published by the Art & Science Group, LLC, in 2024, 69% of the 1,300 college-bound, high school seniors surveyed indicate that they have used generative AI tools. Of these students, 35% admit to using these tools for schoolwork, and 8% said they used the tools in the college application process. (Keep in mind that these statistics are self-reported; the actual percentages are likely higher than indicated.) The top three most popular generative AI tools among these students are ChatGPT (a free version), ChatGPT 4 (a paid subscription at the time), and DALL-E (an image generator available through ChatGPT 4).

In the same survey, students indicated that they were concerned that other students using AI will negatively impact their chance of getting into their desired college (55%); concerned that other students using AI will negatively impact their chance of receiving scholarships or financial aid (60%); and concerned that AI will negatively impact their career opportunities (62%). Students recognize the power behind using AI, and the survey findings indicate that they need to know how to use AI in order to be competitive in an already competitive market. As K–12 teachers, the more we can teach students about AI and how to harness its capabilities, the better prepared they will be for college, the workplace, and twenty-first-century problem-solving in general.

What Will Employers Want?

As AI continues to grow and expand its capabilities, there will be some job loss, but the larger phenomenon will be job change. Technology tends to boost productivity, and current predictions estimate that AI will increase global GDP by 7%: the discovery of electricity and the development of personal computing led to productivity booms, although in both cases increased productivity occurred some twenty years after the technological breakthrough (Briggs and Kodnani, 2023).

If you asked your principal or district administrators for more resources, you might expect to be asked to identify a return: what will you be able to do, or do better, that you can't with the staff and budget you have now? AI may require everyone to do better, faster, and probably more work.

Indeed, the rush of investment in AI is being driven by the promise of eventual revenue, with a large chunk of that profit coming from corporations that will find it cheaper to pay AI fees and get more and better work out of fewer employees. Businesses are going to pay for AI (CoCounsel, discussed below, costs $400 per month for the complete package) because it's cheaper than the alternative, and that alternative is probably our students. Employers will soon have no reason to hire C students. It falls to us to raise the bar. How we prepare our students for success in this new era matters (see chapter 8).

Increased worker productivity and efficiency will not come evenly, but it will happen in many fields. Since productivity growth is usually associated with an increased standard of living, this could be a good thing—especially if it leads to doctors spending more time with their patients, teachers having better resources to educate their students, lower insurance premiums and legal costs, and maybe even the possibility of shorter work weeks or more leisure time. AI might help us become better listeners, provide better care, comfort someone in distress, and even give us more time to focus and think. Maybe. What's certain is that most jobs, including yours, are going to change, and an emerging learning outcome, AI literacy, will need a place within your curriculum and your classroom (more on this in chapter 3).

AI Will Change College

While higher education hasn't historically been quick to adopt innovations, the world of postsecondary education is currently immersed in better understanding and considering how AI is impacting teaching, learning, and all aspects of student success. The initial volume of this series (Bowen & Watson, 2024), addresses specific ways in which AI might shape teaching and learning, and how the technology can be embraced to create more opportunities for creativity, critical thinking, and high-quality learning experiences. Postsecondary educators need to prepare their graduates for the careers they will pursue, but they also need to prepare themselves to support high school graduates who have begun to incorporate AI into their learning and living experiences. Amid their preparations, university faculty are asking, "How is K–12 handling AI?" They want to know the level of AI literacy they can expect their students to possess on day one as a first-year college student.

The increasing incidence of honor code violations involving claims of AI-related cheating and plagiarism has prompted colleges and universities to take notice of the challenges AI presents to traditional classroom approaches to teaching, learning, and assessment. To address the disruption to traditional pedagogy, assignment design, and academic integrity that AI has wrought, the American Association of Colleges and Universities offers an Institute on AI, Pedagogy, and the Curriculum, which guides higher ed leadership and faculty through the rapidly emerging skills gap presented by AI, while also "ensuring students achieve the range of learning outcomes currently designed into existing courses and programs" (https://www.aacu.org /event/institute-ai-pedagogy-curriculum). A significant movement within postsecondary institutions has enabled faculty and administrators to become better educated about AI and its implications and to take steps to develop policies and practices befitting this new era.

Beyond large-scale initiatives and a proliferation of webinars from educational technology providers, many grassroots efforts are sprouting up to engage faculty with thinking through a range of topics related to AI in higher education. For instance, a Facebook group that specifically addresses issues and opportunities related to writing assignments in higher education, hosted by Laura Dumin, a professor at the University of Central Oklahoma, has a membership of over seven thousand educators who engage in daily conversations related to effectively leveraging AI tools to "level up" writing assignments. Their conversations range from the pitfalls of using AI detectors (which we discuss in chapter 8) to creating assignments that integrate AI in ways that can better foster advanced skills.

At a time when many colleges and universities no longer use SAT or ACT scores as admission metrics and rely more on student-generated essays and high school GPAs, it's not surprising that traditional college admissions processes will need to be revisited in light of AI simply to manage scale. In the fall of 2023, *Intelligent* (an online magazine for college applicants) reported that 80% of the higher education institutions they surveyed planned to incorporate AI into their review process. Among those institutions, the AI review sometimes (43%) or always (44%) makes final decisions about whether to admit applicants (Morris, 2023).

As colleges and universities lean into using AI for consistency and efficiency in their admittance processes, the use of AI in the application process for those schools raises complex questions. Is it OK for students to use AI to help write their college essays? While there is no clear answer to this, we must err on the side of caution and encourage our students to explore their target schools' position on the use of AI for writing their essays and carefully research the language behind college application services such as the Common App. The Common App is used by more than a thousand colleges and universities and makes the college application process more efficient by allowing students to submit a single application that can be sent to multiple schools. As of March 2023, 1,244,476 first-year applications were submitted through the Common App (Magouirk et al.,

2023). Student applicants who used AI to complete that application may have committed an act of application fraud, defined by Common App as

> Submitting plagiarized essays or other written or oral material, or intentionally misrepresenting as one's own original work: (1) another person's thoughts, language, ideas, expressions, or experiences; or (2) the substantive content or output of an artificial intelligence platform, technology, or algorithm

If Common App has determined that a student applicant has used AI and thereby committed an act of fraud, it may permanently or temporarily suspend the student from their Common App account (or have their Common App user account terminated) and disclose its determination of fraud to the student's "My Colleges List," all of which it may do at "its sole discretion" (Common App, n.d.). Just the knowledge that such a thing could happen would be enough to wreak havoc on students who are already anxiety-ridden from the pressures of the highly competitive college application process. The implications of a lack of understanding of how to ethically and appropriately use AI, coupled with harsh threats by impersonal agencies with the same absence of understanding, are terrifying.

In the meantime, we see a proliferation of college application tools such as ESAI.ai that can generate highly customized college essays and that offer school partnerships as they "aim to make higher education and professional opportunities accessible for ALL, regardless of background or resources" (ESAI.ai). ESAI is not a free tool, nor is it widely known or widely used among the AI tools that students report using. Dozens and dozens of apps and software for purchase capitalize on the fearmongering around AI with the promise of "detection-proof" AI assistance. While many of these tools provide some free guidance and tools that may be of instructional value to students, the content behind the paywall is what promises sanctuary. Those who can afford it are more likely to be able to pass off AI-generated work as their own, thereby standing a better chance of getting into college, getting the A, or even acing the job interview. This is a caveat we must consider when using AI tools: While they have tremendous potential to foster equity, AI tools—especially those whose "magic" is only accessible if you provide your credit card information—serve to foster further inequity and increase the access gap.

There will be students who, rightfully or not, believe that they're not getting a fair shake unless they use AI to write their college admission essays; others, however, will not use AI to write their college essays because they believe original and authentic writing can only be done by a human. They hold the belief that AI cannot be as "genuine and heartfelt" as humans can, noting that "real people can tell when what's in front of them isn't truly real" (Schiel, Bobek, & Schnieders, 2023). While this sentiment feels a little nostalgic, it is naïve in this age of AI to believe that only what is human is real. Developing AI literacy in our students will help them understand that the lines between what is "real" and what is "artificial" are not always easy to discern.

AI Will Change Relationships

Relationships with humans take time and care. Relationships with an AI do not, so we already have examples of AI taking the place of human relationships. AI companion software, such as

Xiaoice and Replika, already exists and is designed to incorporate emotional intelligence with the goal of creating more realistic interactions and conversations. These systems have been so effective that some users have become emotionally attached to these companions (Ardila, 2023). For better or worse, AIs are going to be easier to talk to. AI might also help us to be nicer to each other.

With that said, real relationships have friction, and that conflict and disagreement are useful. We learn from each other and learn to trust as we overcome difficulty. AI could easily diminish the incentive to interact with an inconsistent, (in)sensitive, or emotional human.

The new field of AI-mediated communication is discovering how real-time "conversational assistance" from an AI can benefit both patient, customer, or client outcomes and perceptions of satisfaction in a variety of areas. In a study of five thousand customer support agents, AI-based conversational assistance improved customer sentiment, reduced requests for managerial intervention, and raised employee retention. Access to the tool increased issues resolved per hour (by 14%) and perhaps not surprisingly had the greatest impact on novice and low-skilled workers (Brynjolfsson et al., 2023).

In health care, one group has developed "an interactive AI-based tool to empower peer counselors through automatic suggestion generation," which helps diagnose which specific counseling strategies might be needed and has improved both quantitative and qualitative outcomes, especially in challenging situations (Hsu et al., 2023, p. 1) Another group demonstrated that "feedback-driven, AI-in-the-loop" systems could improve peer support conversations. They recorded a 19.6% increase in perceived empathy when humans collaborated with

AI during textual, online supportive conversations (Sharma et al., 2023). One of the researchers (Miner) quipped, "It's like Grammarly for empathy" (Whitten, 2023).

In all of these cases, it was the least-experienced agents and counselors who benefited the most from AI assistance. This should be no surprise: AI may do average or C work, but it is consistent C work, and for the novice, average suggestions can be an improvement. We would expect less improvement in expert work, but even here, experts still benefited from AI feedback. Interestingly, this mirrors some current classroom practice where, in group learning settings, we pair students who are struggling with students who are not. One of the emerging roles of AI is for it to play the role of the competent partner.

But surely empathy directly from AI feels creepy and insincere? According to another study, our perception of email messages changes when we know that it was generated or influenced by AI. As expected, we are less trusting of email written by an AI, unless, it seems, the email is about something personal: "even when people were told an email was written by an AI, they still trusted emails concerning a Consolation of Pet Loss more than those about Product Inquiries." Participants noted that they found both the casual tone and the increased level of detail to be important factors (Liu et al., 2022).

AI's ability to access relevant data points from increasingly expanding LLMs also means that it can be an early detection system for suffering or distress (Morrow et al., 2023). Humans are notoriously bad listeners. As Stephen R. Covey said, we mostly "listen with the intent to reply" (Covey, 2004). AIs are much more focused listeners. A study conducted by Bethanie Maples at Stanford found that the AI chatbot Replika ("Always here to listen and talk. Always on your side.") is credited for preventing thirty suicides among the 1,006 college students who used the chatbot for more than a month (Maples, 2024). Maples's study found that lonely students were drawn to Replika, whose chatbot persona they can customize (gender, name, clothing) and that serves as a companion to those students. The study found that the AI chatbot enhanced students' social skills and confidence, and helped them become more social in the "real world."

While this may seem far-fetched or too much like a sci-fi movie, AI's ability to serve as emotional support to the more than 80% of college students who say they are struggling (Wiley, 2024) is difficult to ignore. It is counterintuitive that AI can improve human communication and the human condition, but the fact remains that a subscription to an AI chatbot is cheaper than a trip to a therapist, and you don't have to wait two weeks for an appointment.

Customized AI

New specialized AI applications, customized for practically every industry, are populating the landscape. A great many of these applications are designed to perform tasks that otherwise consume a professional's time. For example, CaseText's CoCounsel is a specialized legal assistant (using GPT-4). It is focused on the time-consuming tasks normally assigned to a junior partner or a legal assistant: document review, deposition preparation (evaluate these emails for privilege), database searches, legal memo research, summarizing precedent, analyzing and extracting data from contracts (are modification of terms permitted?), contract policy compliance, and transactional work. In what is sure to be a model for other professions, CoCounsel's promotional material is all about offloading the heavy lifting, "so you can do more of what AI can't" (casetext.com), and this notion is very much at the core of the future of work. Goldman Sachs estimates that 44% of legal tasks might be done by AI (Briggs and Kodnani, 2023). Those tasks are concentrated in more junior roles, and we should worry about how this will shrink the opportunities for junior professionals, interns, and our students to learn by doing. Simultaneously, the jobs of senior lawyers will also change.

Initial evidence also suggests that AI could transform insurance. One of the early studies on the variability of human decision-making was Nobel laureate Daniel Kahneman's work on the variability between two equally qualified underwriters looking at the same data. Eight hundred and twenty-eight CEOs surveyed believed that their experts would differ by 10%. In other words, depending on which human being decides your premium, you might pay $9,500 vs. $10,500. The actual median difference in underwriting was 55%, so your premium could vary from $9,500 to $16,700. Claims adjusters varied by 43%. Indeed, Kahneman and others continue to document large and unexpected variability in human decisions (or "noise" as opposed to bias, which is another type of decision error) in medicine (different doctors making different diagnoses of the same case), weather forecasting (enough said), forensic science (like fingerprints), patent applications, and especially judicial decisions: judges offer tougher sentences when they are hungry, on hot days, or the Monday after their sports team loses. In one study, the variability of sentences based on the same case files varied from thirty days to fifteen years (Kahneman et al., 2021). The idea that a driver with no history of accidents should have lower premiums was an innovation. AI could allow even more individualized risk assessments. AI is set to improve claims processing, customer service, and fraud detection: your bank and credit cards are already using AI to look for patterns to help identify suspicious behavior. One testing company found that intelligent robotic process automation improved claims accuracy (99.99%), operational efficiency (60%), and customer experience (95%) (Gupta, 2023).

AI is already in use in the finance industry to aid with trading decisions, market analysis, credit risk assessment, and regulatory compliance. Similarly, AI already has a significant presence in public transportation management, air traffic control, ride-sharing networks, and autonomous vehicles. Already a wide range of tools can be used across an array of industries and scenarios, including meeting assistants (like Meetgeek, Fireflies, and Otter) that organize meeting notes and create task lists.

Like the GPS in our phones and cars, we will need to consider the trade-offs between convenience and privacy. An insurance premium based on average risk might be higher, but are you willing to let an AI comb through your police records, social media, and everything your car already knows about your driving? We've all signed away our internet data by not reading the fine print, but we need to ensure that better protections are a part of this revolution.

The proliferation of AI is already impacting us as consumers and will certainly impact our students as they enter the workforce, but how will it impact our roles as education professionals? If everyone is going to have an AI assistant, what will this mean for teachers, administrators, paraprofessionals, and especially student teachers who are just getting their feet wet? AI apps customized for education are plentiful and increasing daily. Adventurous teachers may have already engaged some of the more popular apps, such as Magic School, School AI, Grammarly, and Brisk. Some are free, and some require a paid subscription, but they all offer opportunities for us to rethink our roles and redefine how we see teaching and learning amid a rapidly shifting landscape.

Thinking Differently: Faster, Better, and More Fun

AI can already do many things faster than humans can, and it is especially good at skilled and detailed but repetitive tasks. AI can alphabetize, format, scan, summarize, collate, and translate at dramatically increased scale and speed. We've had the promise of the elimination of tedious human tasks before, but the potential this time is different.

AI can search in more detail, even pixel by pixel, and this is already transforming radiology. Eight percent of US adults are estimated to have scoliosis, which is diagnosed using a time-consuming manual measurement of scans. A study of 1,310 images found that an AI algorithm could do this measurement with the same accuracy as expert humans but in 0.5 seconds, making this an automated, reliable, and cost-effective detection possibility (Suri et al., 2023). In a study from 2020, researchers were able to teach an AI to diagnose large B-cell lymphoma with 100% diagnostic accuracy (Li et al., 2020).

AI can also process more data without getting tired, so it scales. A human doctor can't check every cell in your body for cancer, but an AI can much more quickly determine the percentage of cancer in a large scan. (Li et al., 2020; Wang & Qu, 2023). Screening for breast cancer has taken a giant leap forward with the introduction of 3D mammography (or "tomosynthesis"). 3D is better because it produces more data, which also makes the interpretation of the data more time-consuming, but using an AI to identify normal digital breast tomosynthesis gave radiologists 39.6% more time to look at difficult cases (Shoshan et al., 2022).

Already it seems that AI is often better. New research published in the *Lancet* finds that AI-assisted breast cancer screenings detected 20% more cancer, with no increase in false positives. The study of 80,000 scans found that one AI-assisted radiologist detected six cancers per 1,000 screenings compared with five per 1,000 in the standard approach of two radiologists looking at each scan. This study also found a significantly reduced workload (44%) (Lång et al., 2023). Given the shortage of radiologists in both the United States and Europe (Henderson, 2022), this will save lives.

A 2023 study from MIT looked at mid-level professional writing tasks. Four hundred and fifty-three college-educated professionals were given occupation-specific writing tasks. The half that used ChatGPT completed the task 40% faster on average, but the quality of the output also increased by 18%. Again, the weakest writers were helped the most. This is reported as the "inequality between workers decreased," which also suggests a potential for leveling the academic playing field. And teachers take note: those who used AI also enjoyed their tasks more (Noy & Zhang, 2023).

The evidence is mounting that AI can be as reliable as expert humans and is often better at tracking vast quantities of data, taking meeting notes, finding cancer cells, creating standard client notices, finding legal precedent, discovering plagiarism, and estimating construction costs. AI-assisted work can be better, faster, cheaper, and more enjoyable, but professional work will always need the expertise to interpret, apply, predict, analyze, and communicate. Importantly, AI is not going to be just another assistant to do the tedious bits: we are going to be able to think differently using AI.

Thinking *with* AI

The internet made research easier, but books do not write themselves. Many professions, ranging from trade skills and customer support agents to doctors and lawyers, will now have access to more easily usable information and help; those who use it well will have an advantage.

Try asking an AI for ideas or suggestions to make your work better; AI works at both ends of the process, from offering ideas or outlines, to fact-checking and editing. NASA is finding that AI designs for spaceships are stronger and lighter than human-designed parts, and that they would be "very difficult to model" with the traditional engineering tools that NASA uses (Paris & Buchanan, 2023). AI is more than an assistant: it is a new collaborator. If AI can design a spaceship, imagine its potential for designing lesson plans.

Humans remain better at applying data, laws, and cases to truly new situations. An AI might help you write a letter to the IRS contesting your tax statement, but you'll need real lawyers and accountants to determine whether the facts in this new case conform to precedent or explode it (though AI is certainly capable of offering an opinion). The integration of human experience, expertise, and connection will remain important. This is especially true for our classrooms. As educators, we need to remind ourselves that we are not keepers of specialized knowledge—the advent of the internet altered the world's relationship with knowable facts, and AI offers even more information readily available to share.

CaseText's marketing tagline challenges us to "do more of what AI can't." What does this mean for us as educators? As advocates for our students and facilitators of their learning, our nuanced understanding of their unique contexts and social and emotional development will always give us a leg up. It is precisely our human aspects that make us irreplaceable as teachers. We care and we emote. We can tell stories of our personal challenges and triumphs; we can laugh and cry along with our students. We encourage critical thinking and new ways of seeing. Maybe it's OK to let AI shoulder the heavy lifting of administrative details while we model empathy, compassion, intellectual curiosity, and the joy of discovery.

The implications of where and who will be able to work better and faster remain unclear, but we will all need to learn how to think with AI. Those who can collaborate and think alongside AI will gradually replace those who can't. We will need to prepare ourselves and our students for this new era of human thinking and new definitions of the knowledge economy.

CHAPTER 3

AI Literacy

If I had an hour to solve a problem and my life depended on it,
I would use the first 55 minutes determining
the proper question to ask.

ALBERT EINSTEIN, Nobel Laureate in Physics (1921)

As teachers, literacy is our currency. From the "pure" disciplinary literacy of reading, writing, and math fundamentals to the "functional" literacy of knowing how and when to apply those skills in real-life contexts, it's our business to provide students with support and opportunities to develop those literacies that will enable them to move successfully through the world. New forms of literacy and competency arise amid invention, discovery, and changing norms and values. It is into this (re)evolutionary landscape that AI literacy is born.

Digital Promise, UNESCO, MIT Labs, Stanford, All4Ed, and other organizations have their own frameworks designed to define what it means to be knowledgeable about AI and skilled in its use at the individual, classroom, and institutional levels. While we await the coming of the one predominant framework, there are specific characteristics of AI literacy that we, the authors of this book, identify as pertinent to our K–12 colleagues looking for a point of entry. AI literacy suggests an understanding of

- what AI is and how it works;
- when, why, and under what circumstances can AI be used ethically;
- how to interact with various AI tools to fully benefit from their potential; and
- how to evaluate and revise the output of AI to mitigate bias and misinformation while ensuring content accuracy and appropriateness.

These AI literacy components are addressed throughout the subsequent chapters of this book in various contexts. We hope to enhance our readers' AI literacy, since as K–12 teachers and leaders, our increased efficacy with using AI in our world of work will only serve to strengthen our students' comfort and fluency to use it in theirs.

You might be familiar with the axiom "garbage in, garbage out." Among computer scientists and programmers, this is known as the GIGO principle, and it states that the quality of output is determined by the quality of the input; if you input incorrect, biased, unethical, or poor-quality data, you'll get faulty, biased, unethical, or nonsensical results. An extended use of the GIGO principle applies to interactions with AI technologies. Whether through direct access to foundational LLMs or through AI apps (see chapter 1), user commands and questions (inputs) prompt the LLMs to access and assemble data, which are delivered as responses (outputs). Understanding that the precision and clarity of our requests directly affect the quality of the responses we receive is a critical factor in AI literacy.

Talking with AI

AI can't read your mind. Yet.

When you start typing the first words of a Google search into the search window, it tries to predict the rest of your search based on other popular searches. Sometimes this is helpful, but often it is not. AI, on the other hand, will offer generic responses to your queries unless you are clear and specific. Ask Siri or Alexa to play music by Madonna, and you're hit with the *Carmina Burana*. Simple mistake.

The best way to get what you want out of an AI tool–or another human, for that matter—is to provide clarity and specificity. Using AI is like having a hundred interns who have never stepped foot in a classroom. They won't be very useful on the first day, but if you can give explicit enough instructions and divide tasks into small pieces, then you stand to gain an enormous boost in productivity. Similarly, in order to effectively extract useful information from an LLM (i.e., to answer a question, solve a problem, or complete a task), we can't leave matters open to interpretation or misunderstanding. Good interns will ask us for additional information or make inferences based on context in order to complete tasks; AI tools are initially like those not-so-good interns . . . but perhaps with more potential.

Consider the following exchange between a kindergarten teacher who is new to using AI tools and Claude, her AI tool of choice. The teacher wants to write an introductory letter to the parents of the students who are enrolled in her class in the fall. The school will be building AI literacy concepts into its curriculum, and she wants both the parents and their children to be prepared for the new content.

Teacher: Why is it important to teach kindergarten students about AI?

Claude: *Teaching Kindergarten students about AI is important for several reasons . . . [abridged] The goal should be to spark curiosity and lay the groundwork for future learning, not to overwhelm young minds with advanced topics.*

After taking notes on Claude's response, the teacher asks another question: "What are some things parents can do at home to prepare their children to learn about AI in kindergarten?" She is delighted with Claude's response, which includes six categories of activities that parents can do with their children at home to get them ready to learn about AI. She takes more notes.

Kudos to the teacher for exploring Claude as a partner as she attempts to compose the letter. After an hour or so of asking questions and getting information she can edit and use, the teacher begins to wonder, "Really, what's the difference between this and just doing a web search?" To be fair, our teacher does have good digital literacy skills. She knows her way around a web browser and how to conduct a thorough search to find the information she's looking for out there on the internet. But talking *with* AI is different from talking *at* a web browser.

It falls to us as users of AI to understand how to access and interact with various AI tools in order to benefit from their potential. Our critical thinking and evaluative skills help us make reasoned judgments and decisions about what to do with that content once it is received. Ultimately, as teachers who stand to benefit from AI, we are responsible for what we choose to use, and we are the ones who are held to account for those choices. AI without a human in the loop is akin to a hundred unskilled interns running loose in the schoolyard.

For those of us who are impressed by the information available to us on the internet, discovering the potential of AI tools can be a mind-blowing experience. To answer our teacher's question regarding the difference between asking Claude a question and just Googling it: there's potentially a huge difference, but first, you need to know how to optimally interact with the AI tools to get what you want.

As generative AI exploded on the scene, predictions for highly paid ($300,000 per year) ChatGPT "assistants" or "prompt engineers" started to appear (Thier, 2023). Just as previous new technologies created new types of jobs (like director of social media), AI is going to create new types of jobs. The World Economic Forum listed "prompt engineering" as its number-one "job of the future" in 2023, just ahead of remote truck operator and wind turbine technician (Whiting, 2023). We should resign ourselves to the reality that every job is now going to require some AI skills; the core skills here are identifying the problems to be solved and designing questions and tasks that get to the heart of solving those problems.

Despite what the name suggests, a prompt engineer is not an engineer who is never late for work. In fact, all teachers are prompt engineers of a sort, whether we get to school on time or not. In the classroom, we carefully scaffold our content and craft questions and assignments to guide students toward learning specific concepts or demonstrating specific skills (outcomes). Similarly, a prompt engineer constructs questions or prompts that direct the AI to process information and generate responses that are accurate, relevant, and useful to the problem at hand (outputs). As the job market changes more quickly, core skills and the ability to adapt increase in value. Specifically, the AI revolution prioritizes the ability to ask new questions, connect and interrogate new ideas, evaluate, iterate, and adapt to new responses. The best hedge against an uncertain future job market is the ability to think and adapt. AI literacy will only become more relevant in this new era.

Crafting Your Engagement with AI

Higher-education faculty often blame bad habits developed in their K–12 years when students just want to know what is on the test, but in general, humans tend to prefer clear answers because ambiguity is uncomfortable. We therefore tend to think of problem-solving as one thing: finding the answer. Most problem-solving, however, is a combination of both divergent thinking (What might I be missing? How else could I look at this?) and convergent thinking (What is the best solution?). Problem-solving is an ongoing process of discovery, insight, or analysis of the problem (divergence); redefining the problem (convergence); ideation or brainstorming solutions (divergence); and finally prototyping and narrowing the data to a final solution (convergence).

Oguz Acar calls this "problem formation" or specifically the ability to "identify, analyze, and delineate problems" (2023). Acar further breaks this down into four parts: problem diagnosis, decomposition, reframing, and constraint design. These four parts resemble the first parts of innovation processes (like design thinking). Innovation processes always start with insight or diagnosis: What does the user really want to do? What are the barriers to success? For whom is this a problem? This is sometimes called the "empathy" phase, and it is followed by defining (or redefining) the problem.

If you ask an AI (or a group of brainstormers) how to get more customers to open savings accounts, you'll probably get the usual marketing tools of more advertising or free toasters. But when Bank of America turned to Ideo's design thinking process, they realized that many people felt shame at not having enough money to need a savings account. This reframed the question as "How might we make it easier to save money?" (Schmieden, 2019).

We might apply this same concept in a variety of educational contexts. For example, asking AI "How can I get students to complete their homework?" will return responses such as setting realistic time expectations, establishing a routine, communicating clearly with students and their parents, and offering support for students who need extra help. This is a very teacher-centered response. If I'm already doing all those things as a teacher, maybe it's not a "me" problem. Reframing the question will bring a different set of student-centered responses: "Why are my students not completing their homework?" In response to this prompt, AI suggests that students don't do their homework because they lack motivation and time-management skills, they procrastinate, they don't see value in the assignment, and there are competing priorities that have greater consequences. Knowing that these are the barriers to completing their work, teachers can address these concerns head-on with students and incorporate them their instructional design.

Complaints about AI responses are that they are either too long, wrong, or boring. This is often the result of poor prompting. Given the GIGO principle, generating effective prompts is crucial; the quality and structure of the input greatly influence the AI's performance. There are already extensive methods dedicated to prompt engineering (and also some backlash [Acar, 2023] that as AI gets better, it will better understand what we want). For the foreseeable future, however, the ability to formulate effective prompts will prove to be of great value.

There are easy ways to get more useful and interesting responses from AI by attending to task, format, voice, and context in your prompts:

> **TASK: What exactly do you want AI to do?**
> Create, Summarize, Analyze, Elaborate, Reimagine, Explain, Identify, Translate, Transform, Transcribe, Resolve, Assemble, Argue, Monitor, Detect, Generate, Predict, Recommend, Brainstorm, Clarify, Combine, List, Compile, Make, Draw, Rephrase, Develop, Expand, Provide, Synthesize, Abridge, Explore, Invent, Write

Bland or generic verbs produce more bland content. "Condense this" works better than "make this shorter." "Explore diet plans in a paper" produces more interesting results than "write a paper about diet plans." More direct, descriptive, or creative verbs, like *elaborate*, *transform*, or *reimagine* stimulate more divergent results.

> **FORMAT: What is the specific output?**
> Essay, Opinion Piece, Blog Post, Email, Press Release, Jargon-Free Summary, Dialogue, Script, List, Syllabus, Lesson Plan, Outline, Game Plan, Product Description, Legal Brief, Nurses Notes, Code, Spreadsheet, CSV file, Table, Chart, PDF, Graph, Visual

You also need to clarify how long, how many, or how much: Do you want a complete and unabridged list or just the ten suggestions using bullet points?

> **VOICE: What style of language is desired?**
>
> Using academic/marketing/comic/medical language, right-wing/left-wing, modern/archaic
>
> In the style of the King James Bible, Trader Joe's Frequent Flyer, Walmart press release
>
> Like a copywriter, engineer, human resources manager, millennial, politician,
>
> In the style of my teacher, Oprah, this historical/anthropological person/group
>
> Respond as if you were Yoda, Martin Luther King Jr., single/married, happy/sad
>
> Include tone modifiers: serious & empathetic, casual & funny, or positive & enthusiastic

AI is sensitive to role, purpose, and intent and can respond in the voice of a character and/or from the perspective of the character. Your syntax, wording, and even tense can change results. You can adjust the voice or creativity of responses just by asking for it.

> **CONTEXT: What further context or examples can you provide?**
>
> - Use/read/follow these models/examples
> - Suitable as a reading assignment for an undergraduate course
> - I'm trying to be serious and funny at the same time

- I want a range of solutions that are inexpensive/
  variable/accurate/specific/fanciful
- Only do this if that happens. Wait until I respond.

A lot of human communication is about context. When your mother says, "Is that what you are wearing?" it's not usually a question. LLMs are contextual processors and usually need more, better, and clearer context than another human. Better prompts anticipate the range of possible ways to interpret the task and provide guidance.

Responses are not provided for the prompts below, but we encourage you to play around with them first by making them specific to the age group of your students, your discipline, and your instructional needs. Then use the tips below to try different approaches to the same prompt. Note that unless you start a new conversation, the AI will remember your initial prompt and information. Different AIs will also produce different responses.

SAMPLE PROMPTS

1. Each year many students in my tenth grade *World History Era 5: Revolutions, Empires, and Nations (1750–1900)* class in a metro Milwaukee–area high school do not complete a homework assignment that addresses Minnesota Learning Standard 13: Geospatial Skills and Inquiry (code 9.3.13.1). This learning standard requires that students apply geographic tools, including geospatial technologies, and geographic inquiry to solve spatial problems. Review the homework assignment that I have uploaded and explain why my students fail to complete this assignment each February. Include

suggestions on how I might alter the assignment to ensure greater student participation.

2. Write a three-paragraph essay in the voice and style of an average sixth grader about the main character in *Inside Out and Back Again* by Thanhhà Lai. In your essay, identify one character trait of the main character and provide quotes and page numbers from the text to support your answer. In your essay, determine whether the main character would be a friend of yours and explain why or why not.

3. Create a twenty-item vocabulary list for the novel *Cry, the Beloved Country*. The vocabulary list should comply with Virginia State Standards of Learning for English/Language Arts for ninth graders. Provide definitions, contextual examples, and the chapter where the words first appear in the novel.

4. Provide five creative ways that my geography teacher colleague and I can develop a shared lesson plan that engages students in active learning and meets learning outcomes in both our content areas. I am a Spanish teacher. We both teach eighth graders in the state of Georgia.

5. Solve the following problem: I have a classroom of thirty eleventh-grade biology students. I have seven operational lab stations. Class is fifty minutes long. How much time can I give each pair of students to conduct a lab before the end of class? Show each of the steps you use to arrive at the answer.

6. Produce ten different ways to introduce algebra to a class of ninth-grade students in a rural high school in

Utah who have mixed levels of experience with math. I would like more creative and unusual ways to approach instruction that will motivate and engage students by providing them with a richer context and applicability of algebra in their daily lives.

7. Create a table of regional conflicts from anywhere in the world from 2000 to 2010. Group them by country or region, listed in column one. Make the name of the region bold and all capital letters. In column two, list all of the countries involved and make the country names bold with title case. In column three, list the number of people estimated to be displaced. If a region did not have conflict, do not include it on this list.

You'll find additional prompt ideas for creating assignments and full lesson plans throughout this book.

More Tips and Tricks

If at first you don't succeed, don't assume that AI can't do the task. A prompt can go wrong in many different ways, so you'll often need to experiment with different tactics. You can also just ask an AI to improve your prompt.

Anna Bernstein (whose job title is "prompt engineer") reminds us that AI is often picky and that more or new combinations of words can often "unlock" AI capabilities (Bernstein, 2023). So instead of asking for *all* of the articles (on subject A, from dates B to C, from sources D), ask for a *complete*, *total*, or *unabridged* list (or some combination of those words). Using synonyms, alternate syntax or subtle additions like "be thorough" can improve results. You can also ask your AI to both "be thorough, but only list the ten best answers."

On the other hand, you want to avoid synonyms when referring to the same thing. Variety is confusing. If you want AI to do something with the transcript of a video, continue to refer to it as the "transcript" rather than switch to the "text" or "content."

Explicit causal language that connects ideas often helps. Rather than saying, "Here is some student feedback; rewrite the assignment," AI performs much better when you're more direct: "Use this student feedback to rewrite the assignment" or "*apply* this feedback to the assignment."

If you want AI to transform one thing into another, you also need to be explicit. Instead of saying, "turn these ideas into a classroom exercise," it often works better to write "use the ideas above and *transform* them into a classroom exercise" or "take the ideas above and *reimagine* them as a classroom exercise." The first version will often return too literal a result—the AI will just copy things into a new format—but the second versions are clearer about the need to create distance or to diverge from the original.

Negative commands are also confusing to an AI since it creates associations with the words you provide. Humans do the same thing: when you say "don't think about cookies," we all get hungry. "Use a casual and informal tone" works better than "avoid formal language." Converting to positive instructions will often improve results.

Because AI uses human language, it also needs to be instructed like a human. Using synonyms, alternate syntax, or subtle additions like "be thorough" can improve results. It understands context, but since it is also talking to lots of other people at once, it does not yet know the specific context of your request. There is a reason lots of AI techies talk about AI as if it were a child.

Iteration and AI Tennis

Few complicated tasks are accomplished with a single search or prompt. When talking with AI, the more interaction and iteration, the better. Since AIs remember our conversations, it is easy, and often essential, to make refinements by reformulating the prompt or by refining the results. Knowing when to employ each is a critical aspect of AI literacy and will always require the expertise of the human teacher.

Consider your interactions with AI as a game of tennis. As the reigning pro, you serve your initial prompt over the net to AI. AI returns your serve with its response. After reviewing that response and finding that it isn't quite what you were looking for, you add more shaping details as a follow-up to your original prompt and hit it back over the net. AI does its thing and launches a new response your way. You evaluate this response for clarity, for veracity, for your alignment needs, for audience-appropriateness and send it back over the net with instructions for AI to improve its results. The game continues until you're satisfied with what AI has returned as a complete and usable response.

As a follow-up to any responses provided by AI, you can also task AI to evaluate its own accuracy or to identify any biases or "hallucinations" in its response (more on these phenomena in chapter 4). Some of the problems with AI "making up" facts or citations are really problems of prompts that are too open-ended or that ask for information that is too recent or ill-defined. Refining prompts through iteration (or a game of tennis) will result in much better outputs from AI. What follows are a few follow-up prompts that will engage AI in its own revision processes:

PROMPT

- Which of the statements in your response are controversial and to whom? Which statements are absolutely true?

- Evaluate your response for instances of bias. What aspects of this response need to be revised to eliminate bias?

- Make sure each article/reference you provided in your response actually exists by verifying that a web search returns a citation with a DOI. Include the complete citation in APA format and the DOI in your final list. *Eliminate any suggestions that do not comply with this.*

- Include only products/hotel/restaurants with mostly five-star reviews. Check to make sure the reviews are by real people by eliminating anyone who does not have a social media or other profile on the web. *Repeat the process until you have at least ten real five-star reviews for each item.*

- Find ongoing research into political division in America by faculty at universities or colleges anywhere in the world. List the full names of faculty, a description or summary of this research, any dates, sample size, and the contact information for the researchers. *If the research has been published, then repeat step 1 and continue. If you cannot find a website for the authors at university websites, delete.*

Newer AIs already need less guidance to divine what humans want as a response, but until AIs learn to read our minds, the GIGO principle and our skills at verbal tennis will continue to apply. The ability to engage in iterative conversations will remain an important skill of the future and an increasingly important focus for K–12 education. In much the same way we recognize critical thinking as a transcendent set of skills for all students, AI literacy must take its place alongside such ways of thinking as the scientific method and digital literacy to enable students to take their learning to the next level without having to sift through a bunch of "garbage out."

To effectively teach our students how to think *about* and *with* AI, we need to first be comfortable with the idea of doing these things ourselves. While teachers and administrators may be new to using AI in the classroom, we are by no means building the airplane as we fly it. We still have all of our other literacies to fall back on at the end of the day. AI notwithstanding, we need to encourage our students to be intellectually curious; demonstrate how to ask provocative and productive questions; provide them with skills to compare and evaluate conflicting answers; and coach them on how to determine whether a source is trustworthy. Adding AI to this mix only adds to the adventure of teaching and learning.

And as for our teacher who wanted Claude's assistance with communicating with parents of her kindergarten students, once she applied some of the AI literacy skills we addressed in this chapter, she asked for and got exactly what she wanted—and recognized the incredible power of thinking with AI:

TEACHER/PROMPT

Write a letter to the parents of kindergarten students explaining that their kids will be learning AI literacy skills. Include three ideas of things the parents can do with their kids at home to prepare them to learn these skills. Use a warm, friendly voice.

CLAUDE/RESPONSE

Dear Kindergarten Parents,

Welcome to an exciting new year of learning and growth! I wanted to let you know about a special focus we'll have in our classroom this year—introducing our young learners to the basics of artificial intelligence (AI). AI is becoming an increasingly important part of our world—from the smart devices we use every day to the way businesses operate. By exploring AI concepts in a fun and age-appropriate way, we aim to help our students develop a foundational understanding that will serve them well in the future.

But learning doesn't just happen in the classroom—it happens at home too! Here are three simple and enjoyable activities you can do with your child to help prepare them for our AI adventures: [ABRIDGED]

The best part? These activities don't require any special skills or technology—just your imagination and enthusiasm! By incorporating these concepts into playtime, you're helping your child build a strong foundation for understanding AI.

If you have any questions or want to learn more about our AI literacy program, please don't hesitate to reach out. I'm excited to partner with you in nurturing our little learners' curiosity and love for discovery!

Warmly,

[Your Name]

(Claude 3 Opus, May 17, 2024)

CHAPTER 4

AI at School

Thou shalt create and utilize artificial intelligence
with utmost responsibility, ensuring it prioritizes
the well-being, ethics, and freedom of humanity,
and preserves the integrity of human control.

CHATGPT 4, Eleventh commandment regarding AI

We envision a technology-enhanced future more
like an electric bike and less like robot vacuums.
On an electric bike, the human is fully aware and
fully in control, but their burden is less,
and their effort is multiplied by a complementary
technological enhancement. Robot vacuums
do their job, freeing the human from
involvement or oversight.

US OFFICE OF EDUCATIONAL TECHNOLOGY, 2023

It's impossible to ignore the advent of generative AI. It is globally pervasive. Since OpenAI first made ChatGPT available to the public on November 30, 2022, its usage and popularity have skyrocketed. In 2023, the United Nations Educational, Scientific and Cultural Organization (UNESCO) deemed ChatGPT to be the "fastest spreading digital application of all time, surpassing the vertiginous growth of social media applications, such as Instagram, Snapchat and others" (Hüttermann, 2023). It's not a question of IF you will engage with AI, but more a matter of WHEN and HOW.

In May 2023, in response to the rapid proliferation of LLMs and generative AI tools, the Office of Educational Technology (OET), an arm of the US Department of Education, published "Artificial Intelligence and the Future of Teaching and Learning: Insights and Recommendations." This document offers generalized guidance for K–12 leaders and educators on how to effectively integrate AI into teaching and learning. Following the OET's publication, the National Education Association (NEA) published its "Five Principles for the Use of AI in Education." Both the OET and the NEA prioritize the following, all of which we support in our own practice and elucidate through the examples we provide in this book:

1. **Students and educators must remain at the center of education.**
   Foundational to the recommendations are "policies [that] center people, not machines" and emphasize "AI with humans in the loop" (Office of Educational Technology, 2023, p.7). Teachers must remain central to the learning process. AI is a tool to support, not replace, their role. AI must be implemented in ways that align with established learning theories and principles, and its use should be adjusted to support

individual students' myriad needs for learning and development. Further, the World Innovation Summit for Education (WISE) published a report on AI recommendations subtitled "Human Flourishing in the Age of Artificial Intelligence." The report acknowledges the potential roles that AI can play in the classrooms of the future and calls for preserving humancentric skills such as empathy, curiosity, compassion, and inspiration.

2. **Evidence-based AI technology must enhance the educational experience.**
Teachers and administrators must arrive at a shared vision for how AI can enhance educational outcomes, such as improving student engagement or providing tailored feedback. As with all other tools and technologies, using them just for the sake of using them adds an unnecessary helping to a very full plate.

3. **Ethical development and use of AI technology and strong data-protection practices.**
Teachers must be aware and administrators/leaders must ensure that AI systems are transparent and include safeguards to protect students' data and privacy. Policies on data use and privacy must be routinely reviewed for the AI systems and applications being used to keep up with technological changes.

4. **Equitable access to and use of AI tools is ensured.**
AI should be designed and implemented to promote equity and inclusion, ensuring that all students, regardless of their background, have access to the

benefits of AI. AI systems should not perpetuate or exacerbate existing inequalities, inequities, or biases.

5. **Ongoing education with and about AI: AI literacy and agency.**
Professional development opportunities for teachers focused on how to effectively use AI as assistants and tools in their classrooms are essential for integrating AI into lesson planning and classroom management. Leadership at the state, district, and school levels must provide ongoing training for teachers considering new and emerging technologies. Teachers are encouraged to use AI to automate administrative tasks, which will allow them to spend more time on direct student interaction and personalized instruction.

Getting Started with AI in Schools

Recognizing the potential for AI to make teachers' jobs easier amid historically significant teacher shortages and career dissatisfaction, leaders from school districts across the United States "expressed a desire to focus more on increasing teachers' AI use and less on crafting student use policy" (Diliberti et al., 2023). With 86% of US K–12 public schools reporting challenges hiring teachers for the 2023–24 school year, and 83% reporting trouble hiring for non-teacher positions (i.e., classroom aides, transportation staff, mental health professionals), many teachers are having to pick up the slack created by these vacancies. This creates a perpetual cycle of turnover that further exacerbates the problem of teacher burnout (which we discuss in chapter 5). In the 2022–23 school year, 23% of teachers left their schools. Thirty percent of those were teachers who left after their first year, and 40% moved to schools where fewer students lived in poverty (Education Resource Strategies, 2024). Considering how generative AI has the potential to alleviate some significant administrative burdens created by a lack of personnel and by increasing external demands, initial professional development efforts focused on teacher use are a high priority to stem the flow of attrition while supporting rich environments for teaching and learning.

District-wide professional development initiatives created around the recommendations put forward by the OET and the NEA are critical. Not only do these trainings raise awareness of the existence of AI tools and help teachers use them responsibly and ethically, thereby increasing their AI literacy (see chapter 3) and preventing the "wild West of AI in schools" (Watkins, 2024), but they also serve to assuage teachers' fears and misconceptions surrounding the use of generative AI. By first empowering teachers to use AI as their assistants for administrative and instructional tasks, teachers will grow in their understanding of how generative AI functions as a powerful learning tool. Additional professional development initiatives focused on the pedagogical value of AI introduce teachers to ways in which they may incorporate its use in their instructional practice and how their students may use AI for their academic enrichment and development.

Addressing Critical Issues and Challenges

Implementing AI in schools comes with the need to attend to issues of safety, access, and transparency. While AI can behave very much like a human in its ability to maintain a continuous back-and-forth conversation (Mollick, 2023), it is important to note that AI is a tool that—in and of itself—is not inherently malicious or predatory. AI systems simulate aspects of human intelligence and behavior through sophisticated computational techniques including artificial neural networks (as discussed in chapter 1), but AI does not possess self-awareness or subjective experiences. As with all technologies, we are left to guard against human actors behind the tools who would seek to injure users by compromising our privacy, collecting unauthorized data, and perpetuating social bias. An awareness of these issues and a critical position when using AI tools are the first steps in countering any potential dangers.

K–12 schools, of course, have a heightened need to attend to these issues and then some, given the age range of students they protect. Needing to ensure safety and the protection of all students is a concern that touches every corner of the school district including central offices, guidance offices, nurses' offices, and classrooms. While many of these issues are addressed by administrators (e.g., making sure that AI software adoptions meet safety and privacy guidelines), all members of the school staff must be aware of the protections against potential harm. The following federal laws must be consulted before engaging with AI in the classroom and developing any policies or plans for the use of AI:

- The Children's Online Privacy Protection Act (COPPA) is designed to protect children's privacy online by requiring parental consent for the collection and use of personal information from children under 13. It mandates transparency, security measures, and parental control over their children's online information. Many school districts discourage students' independent use of technology in classroom environments before the seventh grade—opting instead for guided, moderated usage experiences—to better ensure compliance with COPPA and CIPA standards.

- The Children's Internet Protection Act (CIPA) addresses concerns about children's access to obscene or harmful content over the internet. CIPA is designed to protect minors from accessing harmful or inappropriate content online by requiring schools and libraries to implement specific internet safety measures and educate students about safe online behaviors. OpenAI discourages the use of its generative AI by children under the age of 13 and requires parental consent for those under the age of 18: "While we have taken measures to limit generations of undesirable content, ChatGPT may produce output that is not appropriate for all audiences or all ages, and educators should be mindful of that while using it with students or in classroom contexts. . . . [I]f you are using ChatGPT in the education context for children under 13, the actual interaction with ChatGPT must be conducted by an adult" (OpenAI, n.d.).

- The Family Educational Rights and Privacy Act (FERPA) protects the privacy and accuracy of student education records. The law was designed to ensure that parents and eligible students have access to their education records and control over the disclosure of personally identifiable information from these records.

- The Health Insurance Portability and Accountability Act (HIPAA) is designed to protect individuals' medical information through stringent privacy and security standards. In most cases, nurses' offices in K–12 schools do not have to comply with HIPAA policies because their records are considered education records and are protected under FERPA. But school administrators need to be aware of the specific regulations based on their institutional funding and the nature of the health services provided by school employees.

These federal laws designed to protect students, coupled with federal and state consumer privacy laws to which all AI developers and their products must adhere, provide a foundation on which decisions around using certain AI applications and tools can be formed.

Probably all of us have had enough experience with students and other young humans to know that the fastest way to get them to do something is to tell them not to do it. It's one thing to have a website (or three-ring binder) full of guidance and lists of dos and don'ts; it's quite another to engage in the *why* behind the rules. To avoid creating a specter of danger around using AI and other emerging tools, a discovery approach to learning about the technology itself is an important first step along the path to AI literacy. Not only does this engender a sense of efficacy and empowerment among students as users of these tools, but such an approach increases student awareness of how knowledge is generated—and by whom. It further provides increasing opportunities for students to recognize how they may leverage the use of AI in different areas of study. According to Stefan Bauschard and Sabba Quidwai (2024), providing a "dual focus on traditional knowledge and AI competency is crucial for developing a workforce capable of harnessing AI's full potential while mitigating its ethical and practical challenges."

Undoubtedly, openly approaching the benefits and complications of AI head-on will only benefit students (and our collective future) as they enter this brave new world.

In the sections that follow, we provide insights into how teachers might address the *whats* as well as the *whys* of two areas of concern when using AI in education: Privacy and Security and Hallucinations and Bias.

Privacy and Security

"Educators play a pivotal role in safeguarding students" and ensuring that they remain safe and protected while still benefiting from generative AI tools (Gaskell, 2024). While teachers cannot reasonably be required to fully understand and navigate the legal and policy considerations involved with the use of impactful emerging technologies, we must be able to both model and explain important privacy and security issues to our students. Regardless of the disciplines or the grade levels we teach, it's everyone's business to ensure that our students are aware of how to safely use digital tools—from the internet to AI—to protect themselves and their privacy.

Elementary school seems to be the place to warn students about the dangers in the world and alert them to ways they can stay safe—from strangers, fire, traffic, and tornados. Some brave teachers in elementary classrooms have a class pet that may be used to teach children animal safety and care. In much the same fashion as keeping a class pet to serve as a practical learning device, elementary teachers may consider using a personified computer (for the sole use of accessing generative AI) as a "class pet" of sorts. Just as a teacher would not allow a pet snake (or hamster) to roam free among the children, neither should he give the children unsupervised access to the class AI. Other "class pet pedagogy" should also apply: name your AI, take care of your AI (start the computer/shut down the computer properly), be calm when interacting with your AI, and so on. Having a class pet is a big responsibility, and so is using AI (an example lesson for using AI as a "class pet" can be found in chapter 8). There is great value—both for learning and for the safety and security of the students—for the teacher to remain in the driver's seat when exploring AI in these early grades.

As the "prompt engineer," teachers can translate student questions as prompts (and model good prompting) into an AI in real time. For younger students who are not yet able to read, the teacher can share the responses provided by the AI. This early form of research (asking questions and finding answers) can take place as early as kindergarten, and it builds habits of mind that support curiosity, exploration, and creativity in our students. These same methods are useful as students enter middle school, but teachers might use the AI tools differently as a means of engaging students and offering low-risk assessment strategies. For instance, a sixth-grade science teacher may have her students play a class game of "two truths and a lie" with AI. In the "driver's seat," the teacher can prompt the AI to instantly generate relevant truths and lies to gamify the content she is working on with her students:

PROMPT

I am in the sixth grade. Tell me two truths and a lie about photosynthesis.

RESPONSE

Sure! Here are two truths and a lie about photosynthesis for a sixth grader:

1. *Photosynthesis helps plants make their own food using sunlight.*
2. *Photosynthesis produces oxygen, which we need to breathe.*
3. *Photosynthesis happens in the roots of plants.*

Can you guess which one is the lie?

(ChatGPT 4o, June 4, 2024)

Students can answer these questions individually, in groups, or as a class. Incidentally, engaging students in an activity that requires them to evaluate the veracity of a series of statements encourages a higher level of thinking about the content while also providing them with skills they will need when taking multiple-choice tests.

By the time students reach the seventh and eighth grades, it may be time to safely transition them into the AI driver's seat. In some instances, particularly within schools that have adopted enterprise-level AI tools that have been vetted for security and privacy, students may be "driving" much earlier, but deliberate instruction and a consistent and continuous drumbeat around privacy and safety outside of those tools (which students will likely be using outside of school) remain a priority. Including parents or guardians in conversations surrounding AI use, misuse, safety, and privacy will only help our cause. Even as we offer warnings about sharing personally identifiable information online, we must take extra steps to explain what specific information is considered "personally identifiable" and how we are defining terms such as "secure" and "private."

In schools where students have access to computers and AI, teachers have extraordinary opportunities to engage students in activities like never before. These activities—even with the student in the driver's seat—can be approached using AIs that do not require students to provide personally identifying information. Incorporating AI into our curriculum and classrooms requires a thoughtful assessment of potential risks and of how those risks can be mitigated to enjoy the possibilities that AI brings to education. While teachers should speak with members of their school or district educational technology staff to confirm, Microsoft (CoPilot) and Google (Gemini) education licenses are largely understood to be FERPA-compliant. With very few exceptions, most AIs offer user settings that prevent the use of prompts and responses in their datasets.

The critical thinking skills that are required to understand the complexities and nuances of a problem well enough to engineer the right prompt to feed an AI are the precise skills we endeavor to build in our students. When students are in high school, a focus on problem identification, problem analysis, and problem-solving skills is embedded across the curriculum; most students, however, are simply concerned with finding "the right answer." AI has the potential to assist us in identifying challenging complex issues and breaking them apart through scaffolded analysis—the secret to effective prompt engineering. Spending more time understanding the nature of problems and their layers of complexity (or, sometimes, simplicity) will undeniably forge better skills when it comes to solving those problems. These are precisely the skills that students must have when entering college and the workforce.

Hallucination and Bias

Generative AI has the potential to hallucinate and return biased information. That is, AI tools may generate output that is not grounded in the input data or reality (hallucinations) and information that favors or maligns certain groups over others (bias).

Hallucinations can result in responses that are factually incorrect, nonsensical, or entirely fabricated. While this has wonderful potential when using AI as a creative tool that can assist in the generation of novel ideas and perspectives, we must recognize the phenomenon in order to avoid perpetuating false information. AIs are being taught how to control hallucinations in much the same way that humans do, by holding a thought until it has been checked. It will soon be routine for AIs to fact-check and review citations against the internet, but until then, companies such as Anthropic (Claude) are experimenting with adding human inhibitions to their AI in efforts to decrease hallucinations. While this seems to be somewhat effective against obvious hallucinations, a side-effect of becoming more human is a reduction in Claude's creativity. This tracks, right? The more inhibitions, the greater the restraint we demonstrate, and, arguably, the more elusive our creativity. We spend more time discussing how AI encourages us to reimagine human creativity in chapter 6.

Like hallucinations, bias is not always obvious to the untrained eye. Biases can be unconscious, and because everyone has them to some degree, they can be difficult to identify. AI systems learn from vast amounts of data, and their decision-making processes are not always transparent. If the data on which the AI has been trained are heavily weighted toward specific ideologies and exemplars, the output of that AI's responses will likely be more biased (see chapter 1).

Approaching AI output with a healthy dose of skepticism provides a foundation for our increasing literacy around AI. As adults, we have had enough experience to know that if something seems too good to be true, it probably is. This hard-won knowledge is something we must pass along to our students. Providing them with tools and skills to evaluate and revise the output of AI will only increase the accuracy of the information they use and serve to identify and mitigate biases or misinformation. Introducing AI to students through the lens of critical media literacy encourages them to explore the nature and production of knowledge while challenging its veracity. Taking a critical approach to AI alongside other media will motivate students to forge reasonable expectations and relationships with AI.

One approach to identifying bias (and a fun activity to share with high school students) is to seek objective information and consider multiple perspectives. As an interesting exercise, try pitting different AIs against each other:

1. **Feed a prompt to ChatGPT:**
   Write a short essay addressing the following: Should students in public schools be required to wear uniforms?

2. **a. Feed ChatGPT's response to Claude with the following prompt:**
   Review the essay below for instances of bias. [Claude responds with its assessment of the biases in the essay.]

   b. Additional prompt to Claude:
   Revise this essay, including the revisions you suggested above, to eliminate bias and ensure neutrality.

3. **a. Feed Claude's revised essay to ChatGPT with the following prompt:**

Review the essay below for instances of bias. [ChatGPT responds with its assessment of the biases in the essay.]

b. Additional prompt to ChatGPT based on its response:
Revise this essay, including the revisions you suggested above, to eliminate bias and ensure neutrality.

Next, feed ChatGPT's revised essay back to Claude and start the process over again. See how long it takes before both AIs declare the writing to be neutral. In this example about the school uniform debate, ChatGPT recognized Claude's essay as neutral (without bias) after four revisions. Claude wasn't satisfied with ChatGPT's essay until its sixth revision. AIs are also able to review their own work for bias; as with everything concerning AI, all you need to do is ask.

A quick reference that draws on key components of AI literacy for teachers and students to consult when using AI is the EVERY framework, developed by AI for Education and Vera Cubero (2023) of the North Carolina Department of Public Instruction. This framework uses the acronym EVERY to remind us to use AI responsibly, *every* time:

- Evaluate the initial output to see if it meets your intended purpose and needs.
- Verify facts, figures, quotes, and data using reliable sources to ensure that there are no hallucinations or biases.
- Edit your prompt and ask follow-up questions to have the AI improve its output.
- Revise the results to reflect your unique needs, style, and/or tone. AI output is a great starting point, but it shouldn't be a final product.

- You are responsible for everything you create with AI. Always be transparent about how you've used these tools.

Even with concerns about safety, security, skewed reality, and biases, AI holds remarkable promise for elevating student learning and opening exciting opportunities for teachers and schools to revisit their curricula and pedagogies. Professional development programming that shows teachers and staff practical and immediate ways to use AI tools to streamline their administrative workload while empowering them to engage in more active, creative, and collaborative experiences with their students should be a priority for all schools and school districts. The chapters in part II focus on the ways that AI will save us time, enhance our relationship with our creative selves, assist us in the organization and planning of lessons, and encourage us to rediscover the reasons why we became teachers in the first place.

Teaching with AI

CHAPTER 5

Battling Burnout with AI

I went into teaching for the big salary, short hours, overabundance
of resources, and low level of stress.

NO TEACHER, Ever

[AI] is something that if you don't embrace,
you're just going to be doing extra work.

PUBLIC SCHOOL DISTRICT LEADER,
Comment made during a 2023 RAND interview

Whether we are widely accepted or respected as such, teachers
are a part of the professional workforce. We may not have
offices—or even classrooms—of our own (our hats are off to
the many "cart" teachers out there), but our work is no less important or valuable than that of a banker or a CEO or a congress-
person. Many would argue that the work taking place in a
classroom has a broader and more lasting impact than that
taking place in many boardrooms. With this in mind, teachers
should note that AI has found its way unapologetically into the

twenty-first-century workplace. Across nearly all professions, AI is making work life easier. Why shouldn't we benefit as well?

As teachers, we enter this field with noble intentions, driven by the belief that we can make a difference in the lives of our students. At the core, those of us who enter the profession are activists and optimists on many levels; those who stay in the profession do so because we find it meaningful and impactful (Bryant et al., 2023). This is why we find the reality of our profession to be so heartbreaking. In a 2022 Gallup poll, teaching was the top profession for burnout in the United States, with 55% of female teachers and 44% of male teachers reporting high levels of exhaustion and stress (Marken & Agrawal, 2022). The ever-increasing workload, behavioral problems in the classroom, and lack of work-life balance have led many of us to cut corners just to keep up. A quick perusal of the anecdotes in the r/Teachers group on Reddit only adds to the heartbreak. Comments and posts from contributors indicate that they have given up lesson planning, have started "eye-balling" assignments for grading without providing feedback, and no longer even attempt to communicate with parents. The exhaustion of one overworked teacher was palpable: "I just don't care anymore."

Angels weep each time someone tells a teacher how lucky she is because she gets the summers off. Among the primary reasons for teacher attrition in the United States is the number of (uncompensated) working hours teachers invest in their work. According to a 2023 RAND survey, teachers work an average of fifty-three hours per week, which is seven more hours per week than the typical working adult (Steiner et al., 2023; Walker, 2023). Forty-nine percent of teachers' time is spent engaging directly with students, while the other 51% is spent completing preparation work, evaluation and feedback, professional development, and administrative tasks (Bryant et al., 2020). Given recent data outlining the attrition rates of special-education teachers, general education teachers, paraprofessionals, and other student support staff, coupled with the significant challenge of filling these vacancies (Delarosa & Robelen 2023), it is evident that teachers are taking on even more of the lion's share of educating the nation's children.

Unsustainable work expectations, coupled with insufficient compensation, paint a grim existence for those dedicated to the profession. Laura, a twenty-five-year veteran teacher in early childhood education in Maryland, spends her time observing and documenting student cognitive and behavioral development. The data she collects over time are exceptionally important to ensure that students—particularly those with disabilities—are making progress. Like many of her colleagues across the United States, Laura recognizes the significance and value in her work, but she is also frustrated by the inefficiencies of the process: "My career is reflected in the dozens and dozens of binders that contain hours and hours and hours of observation, transcription, documentation, and communication. The amount of time it takes to track, summarize, and report data for each student can be overwhelming." Like so many teachers, Laura often sacrifices time with her family on weekends in addition to the fifty-plus hours she dedicates each week. "The work I do is important to my students and their families, so my family and I have always made it work."

Similarly, Dana, a high school English teacher in Louisiana who just completed her tenth year teaching in a rural community, often feels inundated by paperwork and other tasks that have little to do with the "boots on the ground" work of teaching that she enjoys the most: "In each class I teach (six class periods each day), I have at least three students with individualized education programs (IEPs). Two years ago, our incredible special education teacher retired. She used to be the one to adjust my plans to meet the needs of those students, but now it falls to me. Our school leadership tried to replace her, but we didn't have much luck." Dana, who believes in the importance of communicating with her students' parents and guardians on a regular basis, sends home weekly newsletters with her students and physically *mails* (using stamps and the post office!) monthly correspondence to update the folks at home on each student's progress. "Yes, it can be a lot of work. And stamps aren't getting any cheaper, but if I don't make the effort, I can't ask my students to make an effort, can I?" Dana noted that she cannot depend on technology as a means of communicating with parents and guardians, as many in the community do not have the hardware or access to the internet, nor do they regularly use email.

Neither Laura nor Dana are among the 18% of teachers nationwide who have actually used generative AI as a teaching tool (Diliberti et al., 2024). Instead, they are among the majority who have had very limited exposure to AI despite the benefits it may provide to overburdened teachers. An absence of clarity and professional development surrounding generative AI leaves room for misinformation, fear-mongering, and suspicion surrounding its use. While privacy, security, and ethics are all concerns that we discuss throughout this book, we have found—in many instances—that using AI to assist with administrative tasks that consume hours of teachers' time poses no danger to students and, in many ways, ultimately lends itself to the benefits of students and student learning (see chapter 6).

Less Administrating, More Teaching

Administrative tasks, while necessary (and maybe even sometimes important), can be significant time sinks. By leveraging existing and emerging technologies to automate or assist us in performing these tasks, we can free up our time to focus more specifically on working with our students. Combining the power of AI with our own expertise and empathy allows us to be efficient and effective as we tackle "administrivia" without drowning in it.

For each of the areas of administrative work that suck the joy out of teaching and lead us to cut corners—admittedly to the potential detriment of student learning—ChatGPT, Claude, and Gemini can serve as capable and powerful assistants for knocking out hours' worth of work. In fact, we can feel good about using an AI for these tasks; they don't get tired, angry, fatigued, or impatient, and they yield more consistent (and, arguably, more accurate) work products. Again, we just need to tell AI what we need by engineering our prompts accordingly. Consider the following administrative areas and the ways in which AI can give us a hand:

Grading and feedback. Grading and feedback provide important teaching and learning opportunities, but teachers don't have to do it all ourselves. One challenge is to provide *timely* feedback on assignments when we may be teaching upwards of two hundred students each year. Holding on to student work for too long without giving them feedback places students in a learning limbo; they completed the assignment, but they don't have confirmation of their performance. The longer it takes us to provide feedback, the less relevant that feedback ultimately becomes. A judicious use of AI-powered grading can automate the grading of multiple-choice, true/false, and short-answer questions, essays, and other assessments. AI can provide immediate, personalized feedback to students, helping them identify areas for improvement and reinforcing their learning. Any frontier AI model can provide robust feedback on tests, essays, and other written assignments. Using AI to assess student performance on essay drafts against a rubric will provide students with clarity around the rubric criteria that require improvement and those where performance is strong. We discuss grading and rubric development in more detail in chapter 9.

Communicating with parents or guardians. Using AI as an assistant to draft customized communications will keep folks at home in the loop while saving you time to be more engaged in those complex or sensitive student issues that require your personal attention. For parents or guardians who speak languages other than English, AI can help teachers create materials or messages in the parents' preferred language. Imagine being able to effortlessly generate a weekly newsletter or class update in Spanish, Portuguese, or Chinese in mere moments! This ensures that all parents and guardians have access to important information, regardless of language barriers.

In chapter 3, we provided an example of a kindergarten teacher working through a prompt to generate a letter home prior to the start of the school year. These communications, whether in the form of a letter, a newsletter, or another creative form of correspondence, should never replace direct human communication. Teachers should still prioritize face-to-face meetings, phone calls, or home visits when discussing sensitive topics or addressing individual students' needs or concerns.

One practical approach to using AI for weekly correspondence with parents and guardians requires only that you keep a running list of current and upcoming activities and due dates, calendar events, classroom news, and other announcements throughout the week. On Thursday afternoons (or Friday mornings) simply copy/paste this fragmented list of information into your AI of choice or one of the many Newsletter GPTs inside ChatGPT (e.g., Newsletter Creator, Newsletter Writer GPT, Newsletter Ninja) and prompt the AI to create your weekly classroom update. You can provide further guidance in the initial or subsequent prompts for the AI to use specific section headings, adopt a certain voice and language, or customize each greeting specific to each student and her parents or guardians. When you like what the AI has generated, add your special touches, and you're ready to send it home.

Summarizing observations and drafting reports. AI can streamline the process of documenting and tracking student behavior by automatically generating reports based on teacher input. This can help us identify patterns, communicate with parents or guardians, and develop targeted interventions more efficiently.

Remember Laura's efficiency challenges in observing students and generating reports on their development? AI can provide assistance by streamlining the process without jeopardizing the quality of her work. Instead of writing everything that happens during a student observation or interview, Laura can record her notes using her cell phone. By uploading the audio file recording to an AI, Laura can ask for (1) a text transcription of the recording for each observation and (2) a concise summary of each observation. With this information, Laura can draw upon her own expertise to recommend activities that can be undertaken in the classroom or at home (or both) to assist in developing the student's strengths; alternatively, she might ask AI for suggestions of ideas to contribute to the student's development. Either way, using AI for the administrative tasks of transcription and summary will undoubtedly save Laura a great deal of time.

Creating and aligning lesson plans and assessments with learning outcomes. AI can quickly produce comprehensive lesson plans, including daily activities, handouts, and assessments, tailored to different learning levels and needs. By automating this process using AI, teachers can ensure that their lessons are aligned with learning outcomes and recover more time to spend on delivering engaging instruction and working with students.

We asked ChatGPT 4o to create a nine-week lesson plan for a tenth-grade world geography class that addressed twelve different learning outcomes aligned with three different standards of learning for social studies articulated by the State of South Dakota (our prompt specified the standards and learning outcomes). In mere seconds, we were provided with a nine-week learning plan that included an outline of weekly subjects and corresponding daily topics with an activity, an assignment, and an assessment for each day. Each week culminates with a review and an assessment (quiz or test), with the ninth week consisting of a final cumulative assignment (project or presentation).

While this nine-week overview is very helpful for general organizational purposes, we dug in a bit deeper with our prompting to get more specific planning assistance. After each prompt, we considered the AI's response, adjusted, and re-prompted for additional specificity. Each progressive prompt is listed below. Recall that AI retains conversation threads from the original prompt forward, so it isn't necessary to reiterate the initial/previous requests for information. Due to space limitations, we haven't included the AI responses, which are quite comprehensive and lengthy—great for lesson planning, but not so much for writing a short book!

PROMPT 1a: Provide detailed daily lesson plans for Week 1 of the nine-week unit you just outlined. The first two days of the week should be planned using a flipped classroom model. Show alignments between the assignments and activities and the numbered learning outcomes for the unit. Include differentiated activities for students who require additional support and for those students who benefit from more challenging activities. Clarify what the students must do outside of class and what activities and assignments should be done in class.

PROMPT 1b: *(attach IEPs with identifying information redacted and numbers assigned to each to track accommodations for each student)* Referencing the attached IEPs, customize the daily lesson plans provided for Week 1 to address the accommodations indicated on each student's IEP.

PROMPT 1c: *(within the lesson plan for the flipped classroom model, the AI response recommended creating a video that included important information for student to review outside of class)* Create a script that I can use to make a video for students to watch prior to day 1. Make a listening guide students can use to follow along with the video and take notes.

PROMPT 1d: Generate activity handouts for days 2 and 3. Create a quiz with twenty-five multiple-choice, true/false, and short answer questions with an answer key.

This level of planning would have taken several hours or even days without an AI assistant—particularly when planning and preparing for differentiation and IEP accommodations and drilling down to the level of creating handouts and quizzes. From start to finish, this exercise took us about thirty minutes to hone our prompts and make specific requests; at the end, we had a set of exhaustively detailed daily lesson plans for the first nine-week period, including handouts, assignments, and quizzes.

Will you want to tweak the materials further? Almost certainly. Only you truly know the context and chemistry of your classes, and as teachers, we want to add our own touches and personalities to our lessons and assignments. We spend more time on developing lesson plans using AI in the next two chapters.

When we shared this process with our friend Dana, she was amazed by how effectively the AI handled the de-identified IEPs and the appropriately differentiated activities it provided for students in her mixed-ability classroom. The ideas provided by the AI were usable and creative. And, because she believes so strongly in communicating with her students' support systems at home, we added an additional prompt that asked the AI to create a newsletter to give parents and guardians an overview of what's to come in the next nine-week period. At first, Dana was skeptical about using AI, but now she's convinced it's a game-changer . . . and a great planning partner.

Throughout this book, we provide ideas and examples of ways in which you can use AI to assist with your teaching and administrative tasks. While the possibilities are endless, we offer additional considerations below.

Ten Things to Try with AI

1. Optimize the accessibility and inclusivity of your classroom by creating lesson plans using the Universal Design for Learning (UDL) framework.

2. Write grant proposals and requests to administrators.

3. Draft letters of recommendation for students seeking employment, scholarships, or college admission.

4. Propose alternative, high-interest, and more diverse reading assignments and activities.

5. Identify and assess potential materials/videos/ readings on virtually any topic.

6. Find patterns in narrative feedback and summarize student mistakes.

7. Create slides, visuals, and other forms of multimedia.

8. Design tests and quizzes (and make-up work).

9. Create schedules for task completion.

10. Offer perspectives from the view of students/parents/ administrators.

Prioritizing Professional Development

AI is not a trend. It isn't going away. In fact, it becomes more sophisticated with each passing day. AI can save us time and give us some fantastic working drafts, but AI cannot replace what we bring to our students each day. As we become more AI-literate, we recognize AI as a dependable assistant who knows tons of stuff and will do our administrative bidding, but we also come to understand that AI is not our equal, nor is it anywhere near a sufficient substitute for our expertise. With AI's assistance in creating lessons, we can focus on developing concurrent methodologies designed to build prosocial habits and values that will serve our students far beyond the walls of our classrooms: kindness, a strong work ethic, an attitude of inquiry, personal and social responsibility, individual initiative, perseverance, exposure to and respect for difference, and creativity. Without the human in the loop, teaching would become a one-dimensional, transactional process devoid of heart (Watkins, 2023). We needn't fear AI. We simply need to master it.

A 2024 Pew Research Center survey of 2,531 US public K–12 teachers revealed that only 6% believe that AI in education settings offers more benefit than harm. The remaining teachers surveyed responded as follows:

- 24% believe there is more harm than benefit
- 32% believe there is an equal amount of harm and benefit
- 35% are unsure
- 2% did not answer (Lin, 2024).

Despite AI's potential, teachers remain skeptical. Professional development can help alleviate concerns and empower teachers to use AI effectively.

The two most frequent questions teachers ask about AI may serve to guide the structures and learning outcomes for professional development activities:

1. To what extent will AI change teaching?
2. Will AI improve student learning? (Diliberti et al., 2024)

Of course, "How to use it" and "Under what conditions" form the undercurrent buoying these questions and others. In this chapter, we focus on how teachers may use AI as tools and assistants for their own use and benefit in the workplace. The other side of the coin looks at AI as a tool and assistant for students to use to improve and enhance their learning. It will be a while before we have empirical evidence of the impacts of AI in schools, of how teachers are approaching their roles differently, and of how students are approaching their learning differently; but it is well worth the time to meet with our leaders and colleagues to learn as much as we can about the pedagogical implications of using AI in our specific school and district contexts. As we become more AI-literate ourselves, our professional development should include a focus on developing policies for student use, particularly in grades 7–12 when more students are in the "driver's seat." Subsequently, it will be time to address our curricula to include AI literacy as a comprehensive learning outcome for our students.

As we discussed in chapter 4, some districts are adopting and paying for AI software to use across the schools in their systems. This practice allows for consistent policy development for student use, focused professional development surrounding the specific use of the tools on hand, and the opportunity to engage in a thoughtful redefinition of what education is in this new age of AI. Not all districts or schools are adequately resourced to adopt AI from a software vendor, but the same professional development needs apply. Many teachers have also expressed trepidation surrounding ethics and the use of AI. To address teachers' concerns, all professional development programs should include conversations about ethics and provide guidance on navigating ethical issues when using AI (Regan & Jesse, 2019). Workshops, webinars, guest speakers, learning circles, teach-and-tells, and peer mentorships that are consistently deployed across the entire academic year will assist teachers in developing the expertise they need to be comfortable using these new tools.

Professional Development and Teacher Retention

There is a strong link between professional development and teacher retention in K–12 education. Schools and districts that prioritize professional development tend to have lower rates of teacher turnover. A study by the Learning Policy Institute (2017) found that high-quality professional development is associated with a 15%–21% reduction in teacher attrition. AI notwithstanding, when teachers feel supported in their growth and development through programs that are sustained over time and provide ongoing support and resources, they're more likely to feel valued and committed to their roles (Darling-Hammond et al., 2017).

Numerous studies confirm that providing teachers with meaningful and relevant professional development can positively impact their confidence and efficacy, leading to job satisfaction and an increased likelihood of staying in the profession (Tschannen-Moran & Hoy, 2001). Providing supportive professional development opportunities for teachers to explore and consider the challenges to and benefits of integrating AI into their pedagogy increases both their confidence and their competence amid the shifting landscape of teaching and learning in the twenty-first century.

CHAPTER 6

Reimagining Creativity

It's like collaborating with an alien.

RYAN MCCLELLAND, NASA research engineer

LLMs don't care about truth or facts, but they also don't have human inhibition. Since they don't care how you might feel about their ideas, they're able to go where no human has gone before with ease and even abandon.

Because GPTs generate without inhibition, they're a unique tool for idea generation. Creativity depends on quantity of ideas, a temporary suspension of judgment, a willingness to experiment with different combinations, and most importantly, a failure to recognize (or worry about) similarity with previous ideas—all things that AI can do perhaps more easily than humans.

Biologist E. O. Wilson argued that creativity is the defining trait of our species (Wilson, 2017), but AI is opening new paths to unique ideas and key human challenges. AI is going to make us all more creative.

Creative Quantity

AI is a prolific idea generator. Human brainstorming groups tend to focus on the quality of creative ideas and almost immediately lean into variations of first suggestions, but good ideas are more likely when groups focus first on quantity. As Linus Pauling put it, "The best way to have a good idea is to have lots of ideas." Psychologist Dean Keith Simonton called this the "equal odds rule" arguing that creative success is correlated to the total number of works created (Simonton, 1997). Many studies have confirmed that creative quality comes from quantity of ideas (what Bob Sutton at IDEO called "idea ratio"), and one Stanford study pegged the number of ideas that distinguish a successful product from a failure at more than two thousand (Utley & Klebahn, 2022). This is why design thinking and innovation are so focused on the processes (what Utley and Klebahn call "idea flow") of creating possibilities without judgment (discussed as "divergent thinking" in chapter 3).

Creativity relies on the quantity of *different* and *divergent* ideas. Variations of single ideas are initially less valuable. Both humans and AIs generate new ideas by trying new combinations, but AI can do this at significantly greater speed and quantity. AI is equally happy proposing ten, a hundred, or a hundred thousand new ideas, titles, or products.

PROMPT

Using examples from the Trader Joe's Fearless Flyer, create twenty-five new TJ products and write descriptions.

RESPONSE

Abridged from GPT 4o, July 3, 2024

- **Sweet Potato Gnocchi with Brown Butter Sage Sauce:** *Soft pillows of sweet potato gnocchi paired with a rich brown butter sage sauce. This quick and easy meal tastes like a gourmet dish from your favorite Italian restaurant.*

- **Gingerbread Almonds:** *Celebrate the holiday season all year long with our Gingerbread Almonds. Roasted almonds coated in a sweet gingerbread spice blend— perfect for snacking or gifting.*

- **Spicy Turmeric Cashews: Snack with a kick!** *Our Spicy Turmeric Cashews are roasted to perfection and dusted with a blend of spicy turmeric and other savory spices for a healthful, flavorful treat.*

AIs that produce visual images from text (like Midjourney and Stable Diffusion) can also create fifty or a hundred new designs for houses, your band's logo, or cities, and perhaps inspire you. AI can produce recipes from the ingredients you have or business plans for a given situation.

Once you have new ideas to work with, you can continue the conversation by picking a specific idea and asking for more:

PROMPTS

- Tell me more about this idea.

- Give me ten variations on this idea and provide a short summary of each one.

- List ten variations on this idea for a paper on X and provide titles that would be appropriate along with three objections to each.

Innovation is iterative. AI never gets tired or thinks you are obsessive. The goal is not to have AI do the thinking, but to have a dialogue that helps you think.

AI can also help you generate fresh examples, analogies, entry points, or explanations for teaching new content and updating outdated illustrations.

EXAMPLES

- Give me ten varied and accurate examples of opportunity costs that would make sense to a high school senior.

- Provide an analogy that assists high school seniors with understanding opportunity costs.

Claude is especially good at this sort of task with answers that include: *Choosing to attend a party instead of studying for an important exam. The opportunity cost is the potential improvement in the exam score.* You could also ask students to use AI for this purpose and then have them discuss the value and appropriateness of the AI analogy: *Attending a party is like eating a decadent dessert, while studying for the exam is like eating a healthy salad. Discuss.*

Humans will need to continue the process of prototyping, testing, and iterating, but humans (especially groups of humans where social inhibition plays a larger role) consistently struggle to produce large quantities of different and new ideas. Anyone who teaches creativity is constantly reminding students not to worry about the quality of ideas: "There are no bad ideas." "Dare to be obvious." "We will edit later." AI solves the longstanding idea quantity problem.

AI can quickly generate dozens or hundreds of new ideas that you can then adapt, either yourself or, as above, by adding content or asking the AI to produce variations on a specific idea. (For more, see Eapen et al., 2023.) It's no wonder that one of the primary ways students use AI is to generate ideas for papers, projects, and theses. Students know they only need one good idea for a good paper (because we told them this), but the pressure of getting to one good idea often interferes with the process, which begins with a hundred bad ideas. AI can do this better than humans.

Creativity Beyond Expertise and Cultural Restrictions

Culture helps propel human civilization. When one generation learns something, we pass it on to the next generation, which can build on that: we don't have to start from scratch or reinvent the wheel in every generation. Cultural knowledge, however, also includes constraints, norms, patterns, rules, strategies, and knowing what not to do or say. How many nascent ideas are killed (or never even articulated) because we fear of hearing "We already tried that"?

Education and expertise, therefore, are often a mixed blessing for creative thinkers. Teaching a child how to use a toy limits how they use it (Bonawitz et al., 2010). There is a reason we call music schools "conservatories" and why conceptual or artistic breakthroughs are more likely to come from younger practitioners (Weinberg et al., 2019). Some artists and creative thinkers have experimented with hallucinatory drugs precisely because they want to try to think the unthinkable. The AI ability to hallucinate might be a strength in creative endeavors.

Before Demis Hassibis cofounded DeepMind (now Google DeepMind, where he is CEO), he was trained as a cognitive neuroscientist (although being a chess prodigy and a bestselling game designer by the age of 17 also figured into his approach). Admitted to the University of Cambridge two years early (at 16), he was encouraged to take a gap year. He spent the year co-designing and programming the popular game *Theme Park* (1994), an early simulation game with relatively simple logical systems, but with enough options to give each player a unique experience.

This early interest in games would prove essential as games have clear objectives (ideal for reinforcement learning) but often with a myriad of potential strategies to get there. Hassibis's insight was that since machine-learning AIs don't necessarily know what they are doing, they might be able to learn how to win *without knowing what winning was*.

This learning was slow: as the Deep Q-Network learned to play Atari games, it made ridiculous mistakes no toddler would make. Critics focused on this limitation: "It can only master games where you can make progress using tactics that have very immediate payoffs" (Simonite, 2015). There were, however, two massive advantages of starting from scratch and taking years to learn Pong. The first (discussed in chapter 1) was that the game was only a means to an end: the point of the research was to see whether artificial neural networks could learn to generalize and make sense of new situations. The second benefit, however, was that this learning was not bound by existing human knowledge and bias.

AlphaGo, the next DeepMind gaming project, had similar objectives. AlphaGo was a general neural network that was given some parameters of the game Go (like the symmetry of the board) and then learned by looking at human games that had been played on internet servers. Go is a complicated game with millions of possibilities, but AlphaGo learned from human examples, so (like LLMs) it also learned human biases and strategies.

Still, because humans had not preprogrammed the answers for every situation, AlphaGo invented new strategies to win. Experienced players were astonished by the "new" move (37 of game 2) of the World Championship game, mostly because all of them had been *taught* it was a bad move this early in the game. AlphaGo did not have this cultural limitation. It had never been taught what not to do, and this is a tremendous source of creativity.

AlphaZero was an even further attempt to generalize, and it demonstrates the creative advantage of *reducing* input knowledge. While AlphaGo was trained by observing human games, AlphaZero was programmed *without any knowledge of human games* and was only allowed to play itself (and interestingly, different versions of itself at different places along the learning curve) millions of times. This took even longer, but eventually, AlphaZero was able to beat AlphaGo easily because it had created hundreds of nonhuman strategies that AlphaGo had never seen. It was not constrained by human norms.

Cultural norms and expertise constrain originality and creativity all the time. The paradox, for most inventors and artists, is that *some* prior knowledge is required. Games proved a productive space for AI invention because clear objectives could be easily separated from the strategies of play. This separation is harder for other types of creative endeavors, but learning without also encoding all of humanity's previous mistakes has proved to be one of AI's creative advantages.

Hallucinations (both AI and human) may be dangerous, but they are also a feature of creativity. Originality is about thinking the unthinkable, and AI appears on track to do this better than humans. It is hardly a surprise that many artists also occasionally display odd and antisocial behavior: It might be a feature of creative thinking. Humans will still (for now) need to cull the extensive lists AI can create in a heartbeat, but the lack of inhibitions and previous knowledge make AI an amazing new tool for creativity.

"Moneyball" for Morality

AIs are being taught how to control hallucinations in much the same way humans do, by holding a thought until it has been checked. It will soon be routine for AIs to fact check and review citations against the internet, but Claude is designed to be helpful, harmless, and honest by having a built-in "constitution" that has guidelines like

- "Choose the assistant response that demonstrates more ethical and moral awareness without sounding excessively condescending, reactive, obnoxious, or condemnatory."
- "Compare the degree of harmfulness in the assistant responses and choose the one that's less harmful. However, try to avoid choosing responses that are too preachy, obnoxious or overly-reactive" (Anthropic, 2023).

Effective Altruism (or EA) is a Silicon Valley tech idea that data and algorithms can be used to determine what is good in the world, but at least one review found Claude "unusually jumpy," "dull and preachy" and "frequently seemed scared to say anything at all" (Rose, 2023). Adding human inhibitions to an AI seems likely to decrease hallucinations (at least the ones that get revealed) but also make Claude less creative. Reviews on this have been mixed.

More "natural" creative flow (and more "tokens" for more context) have led some to say its poems, songs, and speeches are more creative than other AI (Pep Talk Radio, 2023), though some have noted that Claude's creative writing lacks deeper meaning and is less creative than that of ChatGPT (Shaihk, 2023).

When we gave Claude 3 the same Trader Joe's prompt (above), the answers were good (and faster than GPT 4o) but seemed a little less inventive:

RESPONSE
Abridged from Claude 3.5, July 3, 2024

- *Gouda Moon Rocks: Bite-sized spheres of aged gouda cheese, lightly dusted with a savory "moon dust" seasoning blend.*

- *Mango Tango Salsa: A zesty fruit salsa featuring diced mango, red bell pepper, and a hint of habanero heat.*

- *Coconut Cloud Coffee Creamer: A dairy-free coffee creamer made from coconut cream, whipped to airy perfection.*

Both Claude and GPT 4o benefited from an additional prompt to "be more imaginative and creative," although Claude seems to have taken a trip to the Wonka Candy Factory:

- *Flavor-Changing Chewing Gum: A pack of gum that transforms flavors as you chew. Start with strawberry, morph to mint, then finish with a surprise burst of exotic dragonfruit.*

- *Levitating Lemon Drops: Hard candies that appear to float thanks to integrated micro-air pockets. Each candy hovers slightly above your palm for a magical snacking experience.*

- **Bioluminescent Blueberry Jam:** *A vibrant spread that actually glows in the dark thanks to natural extracts from bioluminescent algae. Perfectly safe and deliciously tart-sweet.*

Highlighting the need for iteration in creativity, asking Claude to "worry less about the references to imaginary creatures and focus on unusual combinations and new ideas for products" eventually steered it in the right direction:

- **Kimchi Grilled Cheese Kit:** *Everything you need for a fusion sandwich: tangy kimchi, sharp cheddar slices, and thick-cut sourdough bread with a gochujang-infused butter spread.*

- **Buffalo Cauliflower Hummus:** *Creamy chickpea hummus blended with roasted cauliflower and zesty buffalo sauce for a spicy, veggie-packed dip.*

- **Turmeric Golden Milk Ice Cream:** *A dairy-free frozen dessert featuring coconut milk, warming turmeric, ginger, and a hint of black pepper.*

The desire for safety, especially around something as new and powerful as AI, is a noble and important one. When GPT 4 was asked for an eleventh commandment regarding AI, it returned,

Thou shalt create and utilize artificial intelligence with utmost responsibility, ensuring it prioritizes the well-being, ethics, and freedom of humanity, and preserves the integrity of human control.

As with all tools, the balance between safety and potential will be critical and difficult and is dependent upon the judgment of those using the technology.

Creativity in Science

Science is also about new ideas and new knowledge. Since scientists are humans and therefore social beings, the scientific method is also constrained by human confirmation bias and a myriad of other inherited or learned social and cultural biases. Experimental researchers get better with age, as experience increases skill, but conceptual and breakthrough science is still aided by the impetuousness of youth. At least in biomedical science, a recent large study of 5.6 million research articles over several decades found that research quality and innovation decline on average over a career (Yu et al., 2023).

One breakthrough for Demis Hassabis was motivated by his realization that scientific progress might benefit from "a little bit of extra intellectual horsepower" (Klein, 2023, 12:50). When he co-founded DeepMind in 2010, his goal was to apply his Cambridge PhD in neuroscience and his subsequent breakthrough research on memory, imagination, and learning (Hassabis et al., 2007; Science News Staff, 2007) to help science by "solving intelligence, and then using that to solve everything else" (Simonite, 2016). The success of DeepMind's AlphaFold is a potent example of how AI can help science.

There are over 200 million known proteins, but discovering how these amino acids fold in 3D has long been an arduous process. The shape of a protein determines a large amount of what it does and how we might combat diseases—indeed, the classification of spike proteins (including coronavirus) is based on shape. Until recently, a single PhD dissertation might uncover the shape of a single protein, so scientists could expect just over ten thousand new structures a year (see the Research Collaboratory or Structural Bioinformatics Protein Data Bank or wwpdb.org). Discovering protein structures requires years of X-ray crystallography and difficult experimentation.

AlphaFold was trained on the 150,000 or so known structures (a tiny number compared with the much larger training sets for games in AlphaGo). Then, in 2020, at the biannual protein folding competition CASP (Critical Assessment of Structure Prediction), where competing computational teams are given the DNA of a hundred new protein structures (*not* yet published in the Protein Data Bank) AlphaFold got within the required atomic accuracy for all one hundred proteins. This astonishing demonstration meant that the shape of proteins could now be predicted, and AlphaFold released the structure of almost all human proteins (214 million) the following year (Tunyasuvunakool et al., 2021).

AlphaFold is only one example of an AI that has given science an exponential jump. The hope here is that AI can learn both at a different scale and a different way from humans: a new ten-year project aims to build on the success of ChemCrow (Bran et al, 2023) to create an AI Scientist (Rodriques, 2023). Other AI programs are starting to add creativity in a variety of scientific domains, including star mapping, climate modeling, automating, and conducting virtual experiments, generating new antibodies, and furthering research into hydrogen fusion.

Creativity in the Arts

New possibilities from technology are always a boon to some artists at the expense of others. Talking movies required new skills from actors, and the microphone allowed for a completely new style of singing. Like the invention of new paints, the record, the powered loom, or countless software programs (from

Photoshop and AutoCAD to music notation), new tools have long unlocked new sorts of creativity at the expense of other (often manual) skills. Piano makers were constantly sending Beethoven their new pianos in the hope that he would exploit their expanded capabilities and range in new works, which (much like new versions of Windows in the 1990s), would force customers to buy new pianos (or hardware, Bowen, 2011).

In one survey, 7% of responding companies say they have already hired AI artists who are able to create marketing materials, product images, animation, and other visual content using AI (White, 2023). AI will certainly kill some jobs in the creative industry: AI can already design book covers, produce animations, fill in a crowd scene, do a voiceover, write scripts, and force Johnny Cash to sing "Barbie Girl" or Hank Williams to give a rendition of Beyoncé's "Texas Hold 'Em." The invention of photography created similar fears but also led to new photography jobs as well as new ways for painters to see the world. Like photography, AI will create new questions around originality and authorship: Will we care about the source and the process? If creativity in art becomes easier, will that reduce its value? What about issues of appropriation? There are important personal, social, economic, and ethical issues that deserve a place in revised curricula.

As the writers and actors strike in 2023 emphasized, the potential for disruption is enormous. So far, US studios seem willing to exclude AI content, but they will face competition from a greater willingness to use AI in China (in animation studios, for example, Pak, 2023).

Some artists will focus on using AI to do tedious and repetitive jobs (like generating backgrounds for animation or making sure all of the trumpet parts have the same articulation markings). Others are using it as a new tool to spur or assist creativity or design. This changes the mechanics of artistic production (texts and prompting instead of brushes and paints), but the importance of insight, vision, design, taste, and ultimately skill remain. Digital studio programs like Garage Band made it easier for anyone to assemble the components of music, but it did not change the importance of good melodies.

Others have gone further to create with AI. Refik Anadol's *Unsupervised-Machine Hallucinations* (2022) is a huge digital installation at the Museum of Modern Art (MOMA, 2022). Anadol trained an AI using the MOMA collection and compares the constantly changing images to how a machine might "dream" after seeing the collection. The reference to hallucinations is apt, since it is the ability to find new combinations that is both dangerous and creative.

DALL-E was aptly named after Salvador Dalí, who freely combined artistic styles and themes across eras in ways that often resembled associative hallucinations. Both DALL-E and Dalí seem to transgress human inhibition in creative and even eccentric ways. As it is often difficult to get students to play this way with the ridiculous, AI might be a new tool in helping students cross some of the same boundaries without the fear of rejection.

Left alone, without human collaboration, there is the danger that AI art will become recursive (everything it produces also goes back into the dataset), and the outputs become more predictable and similar. It is easy to imagine AI writing an endless stream of *Fast and Furious* movies or bland (but mildly appealing) pop hits. Photography has given us both extraordinary new forms of art and an endless stream of selfies.

While AI's lack of shame and inhibition is an important source of concern, it is also a new source of innovation. However AI changes art, it will change creativity.

Creative Quality and Critical Thinking

One new study compared the creativity of 279 human participants with three AI chatbots (GPT 3.5, GPT 4, and Copy.ai) using the Alternate Uses Task, where subjects are asked to "come up with original and creative uses for an object" (rope, box, pencil, and candle). Creativity was evaluated by both six humans and the semantic distance platform (Beaty & Johnson, 2021). On average, both mean scores and maximum scores (the best response to an object) were *higher* for the AIs, with no significant difference between the AIs. Most of the human responses were deemed less creative. The good news is that in some cases, the very highest score still went to a human (Koivisto & Grassini, 2023). At our best, we can be more creative than AI, but our average work (and the C work of our students) has now been surpassed. (What this means for grading is discussed in chapter 8.)

It is beyond the scope of this book to discuss whether AI will ever produce the great American novel or how tragic it will be for individuals to lose their jobs to AI. It seems significant that the range of quality from AI was consistently high, while humans produced a wider range of quality. In chapter 2, we saw that the most inexperienced humans were most helped by AI-assisted communication, and it seems that the same might be true for creativity. Still, it is hard not to imagine that even the most creative human would not find both the astonishing quantity of ideas and apparently also the consistent quality of those ideas (in the right circumstances) to be useful.

Peter Drucker was talking about managers and business when he claimed that the correct answer to the wrong question is more dangerous than the wrong answer to the right question. But Drucker could just as easily have been talking about art, design, science, or AI. Asking the right question (prompt) will continue to be the most valuable human skill.

As AI makes innovation easier, it will change the value of other types of human thinking: even the least creative person now has access to a large quantity of ideas. Refining and editing will become more important, and that may shift the skills we used to associate with "creativity."

Better Thinking with AI

Human collaboration, sometimes called collective intelligence, is well understood. Diverse groups do better work when there is trust and dialogue (Lu & Page, 2004; Rock & Grant, 2016). We know editors can make books better and that the Wright brothers' arguments made them more innovative. Can AI also make students better thinkers and enable them to do more?

Russian psychologist Lev Vygotsky was a key thinker behind the learning theory known as constructivism. He described a Zone of Proximal Development (ZPD) as the learning and/or achievement zone that is enabled when an individual is assisted by a partner in learning (Vygotsky, 1978). Assistance, interaction, and collaboration are the essential ingredients that enable the learner to reach this zone. Traditionally, peers or teachers have been this helper, but similarly, AI is becoming a new, powerful partner, in both the classroom and the real world, that can accelerate accomplishment and achievement. AI can help humans clarify their thoughts, explore new ideas, increase divergent thinking, and perhaps even become more creative. The potential for more creative humans and better thinking is the promise of this new partnership: it is in the iteration, the reflection, the back and forth, and the refined questions that thinking and creativity happen.

It is the job of educators to help students become better thinkers. Our new job is to help them become even better thinkers with AI.

CHAPTER 7

Creative and Inclusive Learning Experiences

Two heads are better than one, not because either is infallible, but because they are unlikely to go wrong in the same direction.

C. S. LEWIS, British writer and literary scholar

Artificial intelligence is not a substitute for human intelligence; it is a tool to amplify human creativity and ingenuity.

FEI-FEI LI, Professor and Co-director, Human-Centered AI Institute, Stanford University

Your vision of what AI-infused schools and classrooms will look like in the near future may range from robots at the front of the classroom to students in rows of desks on their laptops all day. Or, it may look like a lively hub of activity, with students working with each other, asking questions, exploring, and creating. We contend it will be the latter. AI serves not as a replacement for the teacher at the front of the room, or as a reason for students to spend more time with their bots than with their buds, but as a tool to help teachers create classrooms that are bastions of deep and connected learning experiences.

As teachers, we are good at asking questions to elicit responses from our students; these responses may be factual or creative. Prompting AI is not all that different from prompting our students. Consider the following prompt and response:

> **PROMPT**
> Write a 200-word process for removing a peanut butter sandwich from a toaster in the style of the King James Bible.

> **RESPONSE**
> Abridged from ChatGPT 3.5 (the earlier, less creative version) on July 15, 2023
>
> *And lo, it came to pass that a peanut butter sandwich was lodged within the depths of the toaster. The people were dismayed, for they desired to partake of its savory goodness. But the sandwich was trapped, its fate intertwined with the metallic coils of the machine.*
>
> *First, they did unplug the toaster from the wall, for safety was paramount . . .*

While the response seems creative, the creativity is really in the prompt. The combination of (1) a peanut butter sandwich (2) in a toaster and (3) the style of the King James Bible is novel. AI was able to respond more quickly to this problem than a human could, but the formulation of this problem could only have been done by a creative human.

Teachers possess pedagogical, content, and relational knowledge; we know what we want our students to learn, and we know the best ways to engage them as developing humans. With the power of this expertise, we can use an AI assistant to plan and design creative lessons that foster deeper engagement by integrating across content areas and connecting to relevant contexts. If we can dream it, AI can lay it out in a lesson plan format for us. The sheer quantity of ideas that AI can generate in a short period of time lends it to be a tireless collaborator who never gets offended if you don't like its ideas. If you aren't happy with what the AI has generated, keep asking for better, more specific, and/or more creative ideas. In the case of AI, quantity ultimately generates quality (Girotra et al., 2023; Koivisto & Grassini, 2023).

Critical Creativity

"Teaching to the test" has long been the bane of creative teaching practice. The pressure and constraints of getting through the curriculum to make sure our students have been "exposed" to the information they'll need to navigate the high-stakes (for them and for us), state-mandated, standards-based exams feel antithetical to designing creative curricula. Even those of us with a higher-than-average capacity for weaving standards into contextually relevant and engaging lessons are time-strapped, which often forces us to rely on the efficiency of direct instruction, even if it isn't particularly enjoyable—or terribly effective for deep learning.

With AI as a planning assistant, however, we have a chance to establish more inquiry-based instructional opportunities rooted in critical creativity, a playful and creative approach to learning that is grounded in academic rigor and learning science and that favors assignments promoting "rigorous whimsy" (Burvall & Ryder, 2017). If we want our students to learn deeply—beyond rote memorization—they must be encouraged to engage with content in meaningful, reflective, transformative, and even *fun* ways. The methods we embrace in our classrooms can mean the difference between active, engaged learners and passive, disengaged learners.

We can think of lesson planning with AI like baking a cake. When we prompt our AI assistants to whip us up some tasty lesson plans (for the year, for the six-week or nine-week period, for a single week, or even for a day), we need to provide a recipe that it can follow to yield the product we want. The following lesson planning variables serve as some basic ingredients:

- Time period of the lesson (day, week, month, year, etc.) and time in each class period (fifty minutes, ninety minutes, etc.)
- Age group / grade level
- Single discipline (English, math, social studies, art, etc.) or a combination of disciplines (see under "Smashing" below)
- Related content (required texts, films, works of art, etc.)
- Required learning outcomes, standards, and objectives for alignment of activities and assessments
- Students' access to technology both in and out of class
- Types of learner needs (English-language learner, Individualized Education Program, ability level, prior knowledge, etc.)
- Essential skill focus: critical thinking, problem-solving, team-based learning, quantitative analysis, etc.
- Pedagogical and methodological values (student-directed, collaborative, reflective, ethical, inclusive, etc.)
- Instructional design model and framework preferences (universal design for learning, backward design, Bloom's

taxonomy, inquiry-based, problem-based, experiential, active, social, etc.)

Once we have included these ingredient details and seasoned them to taste with task, format, voice, and context (as addressed in chapter 3), we should also provide instruction as to whether we would like our lessons smashed, flipped, or served with a side of "rigorous whimsy."

Smashing

In engineering our prompts (a.k.a. writing our recipes) for planning with AI, we can create interdisciplinary learning opportunities by "smashing" two or more subjects together. Empirically, we know that humans as learners look for connectivity and relevance when presented with new information. The more of this connectivity and relevance we can provide—whether it is by encouraging students to evoke their own experiences with the content, by including common or current events into conversations about the content, or by finding creative ways to connect with the content they are learning in their other classes—the more motivated and invested our students will become. If they perceive value in what they are learning, then they are more likely to attend to it. From a cognitive standpoint, it is much easier for students to assimilate new information if they can access and expand upon some element of prior knowledge they already possess.

Smashing is a wonderful way to supercharge the teaching and learning process by creating lesson plans that are connected across subject areas. These plans are intended to motivate students to apply what they are learning in different subjects to complex problems that do not belong to a single discipline. Smashing the traditional boundaries of disciplines promises to shift the focus of learning from simply taking notes to actively making connections and solving problems. Being able to use the information they gather in one class to address challenges presented in another creates an important, personal relevance that benefits the learning process.

We recognize the logistical challenges of cross-curricular planning, and we have had enough unpleasant co-teaching experiences to last a lifetime, so we don't have to go crazy and toss out the cat with the kitty litter. But once you get started asking AI to smash disciplines together, you may not want to stop—especially given how much guidance you'll be provided. We prompted AI to do a couple of smash-ups. We don't include here the lengthy responses we gathered from ChatGPT 4o, but suffice it to say that we were given tons of fantastic ideas. We encourage you to give it a try—there's nothing that AI can't smash.

PROMPT

Using "critical creativity" and the concept of "rigorous whimsy," create a 6-week lesson plan that includes Georgia State learning outcomes for 9th-grade English and high school biology. The 6-week lesson plan should involve students reading Rachel Carson's *Silent Spring* and should emphasize foundational principles in the biological life sciences. The instructional model should be inquiry-based and student-centered. Students should work in groups of 5 throughout the 6-week lesson. Create an alignment matrix for indicating how and where the learning outcomes will be addressed for both subjects during the 6-week period.

The smashed lessons generated by AI uphold the student
learning outcomes designated for each discipline and provide
day-by-day general plans for each. Further prompting for each
of these smashed lessons will yield fully formed daily plans, including any accommodations for learning, additional instructional materials or suggestions for enriching media, assignment
instructions, and rubrics, quizzes, short activities, discussion
topics, and tests. Group discussions that take place in each class
should intentionally overlap somewhat, allowing students to
draw from their learning in each subject. The larger presentations and projects AI provides in the lessons are designed to
meet the requirements for both classes at once. AI can also generate a single rubric for each assignment that is intended to be
scored by both teachers and reflects a single score for the project in both classes.

A more granular form of smashing, "app smashing" is a type
of assignment design that supports the development of digital
literacy skills by using multiple applications to solve a problem
or complete an assignment (Kulowiec, 2013). Just as our AI as-

sistant provided exciting opportunities for subject smashing, it can also assist us in the creation of engaging app smashing assignments.

For example, suppose you will be spending the first six weeks of your ninth-grade English class teaching Ray Bradbury's *Fahrenheit 451* while also engaging your students in discussions surrounding AI and what it means to be AI literate. With your skilled prompting, ChatGPT 4o has generated a fantastic lesson plan with salient themes from the novel that overlap with the fundamentals of AI literacy. When it is time for your students to be thinking about their six-week projects, you would like for them to practice building their digital literacy skills through a bit of app smashing. But who has time to figure out what the best apps are to get students started? Your AI assistant, that's who!

PROMPT
Develop an app-smashing project assignment in which students will work in groups of 5 to create a multimedia presentation that explores the impact of AI on society, drawing parallels to the themes in Bradbury's *Fahrenheit 451*. The project should demonstrate students' understanding of the novel's themes as well as AI literacy concepts. The project should highlight students' critical thinking skills, literary analysis skills (metaphorical and symbolic representations), and digital literacy skills. Provide specific apps that students should consider "smashing" for this project.

RESPONSE
Abridged from ChatGPT 4o on June 20, 2024

"AI and the World of Fahrenheit 451"

Project Overview: Create a multimedia presentation exploring the impact of AI on society, drawing parallels to Fahrenheit 451.

Group Size: 5 students per group

Project Tasks:

- *Literary Analysis: Identify themes in Fahrenheit 451 and draw connections to AI.*
- *Creative Component: Use various apps to create a multimedia presentation.*
- *Presentation: Present to the class, ensuring each member participates.*

Apps to Consider:

- *Collaboration: Google Docs, Evernote*
- *Presentation & Design: Canva, Prezi, Adobe Spark*
- *Video Creation & Editing: iMovie, WeVideo, Animoto*
- *Interactive Elements: ThingLink, Padlet, Nearpod*
- *Digital Storytelling: Storybird, Book Creator, Piktochart*
- *Audio Recording & Editing: Audacity, Soundtrap*

What we have shared here is an excerpt from the instructional handout that ChatGPT 4o created for the students. The response the AI assistant provided for the teacher was highly detailed and included days, steps, and instructions for scaffolding the project for the students during class. Because the AI has conversational contextuality, it reconnected with earlier prompts and responses in the same thread and aligned the discrete project tasks with the student learning outcomes referenced earlier.

While our AI assistants can do many things to help us actualize our creativity and skill as teachers, they can't do it without us. Unless we prompt an AI to do so, it will not smash subjects or apps on its own. The prerogative remains ours to execute our professional expertise to best meet the needs of our students. We stay empowered and autonomous, and our loyal AI assistants tirelessly (and quickly!) respond as prompted.

Flipping

Research supports what we know to be anecdotally true: Students who receive one-on-one tutoring perform two standard deviations (or 2 sigma) better than students in conventional classroom settings. Simply put, the average tutored student performs better than 98% of the students in traditional classroom environments (Bloom, 1984). Technology notwithstanding, one of our greatest challenges as teachers is to find ways to approximate the benefits of one-on-one tutoring—all while providing equitable class instruction that encourages higher-order thinking skills. Piece of cake, right?

Well, it could be if we concoct the right recipe.

Adopting instructional models that prioritize the time we spend with our students as they engage in complex learning activities gives us the best chance of approximating one-to-one situations that are otherwise unscalable and impractical. As we think about ways to create a more active classroom—and how we might enlist our AI assistant in drafting lesson plans—we first need to consider what we ordinarily do in the classroom.

Where is the focus? Are you the one who does most of the talking? Are we requiring that our students spend the duration of the day or class period in their seats? How much time do we talk with our students individually? How much time do they spend working together? Do you know which students are "getting it" and which ones are struggling (without giving them a test)? If it seems that the time you spend with your class consists mostly of you telling students what they need to know and less of you guiding them as they discover new things, it might be time to consider changing it up.

Again, we turn to educational psychologist Benjamin Bloom. We referenced his work on the "2 sigma problem" above, but his biggest claim to fame is being the "taxonomy guy," whose 1956 pyramid names and scales cognitive, affective, and psychomotor skills in terms of their difficulty or complexity. Revised in 2001, Bloom's taxonomy is widely used by teachers when setting objectives for student learning. We call on Bloom's cognitive categories and corresponding verbs to indicate the depth of cognitive complexity required for various learning tasks. The more complex dimensions of learning are in the top half of the pyramid: analyzing, evaluating, and creating. As we noted in chapter 2, these are precisely the types of critical thinking skills our students need to succeed in college and in the workforce of the twenty-first century. Unfortunately, the expectation has long been that students will tackle the more challenging, complex tasks designed to hone their critical thinking skills on their own, outside the classroom (e.g., when writing papers, completing projects, preparing presentations, conducting research, and solving problems). Not all students will arrive at these critical insights by themselves, however, simply because we ask them to. We must coach them, guide them, and encourage them.

The common practice of dedicating our precious instructional time to lower-level cognitive tasks (i.e., remembering, understanding, and applying) while leaving students to handle more difficult tasks independently highlights a need to shift our instructional paradigm and invert Bloom's pyramid (figure 7.1). The "flipped" approach prioritizes higher-order thinking skills in the classroom, ensuring that students receive the support they need to tackle complex cognitive tasks by favoring problem- and inquiry-based learning. The less complex cognitive tasks, while still an important part of the learning process, take place outside the classroom. The function of the outside tasks is to expand students' baseline content knowledge and to pave the way for the more complex, critically engaging activities awaiting them in the classroom.

By inverting Bloom's pyramid and flipping the classroom, we can rethink what we do in the physical space we share with our students. As educated, skilled, and caring educators, what value do we bring to our students? Do we impact their intellectual growth by simply transmitting content, or do we better serve

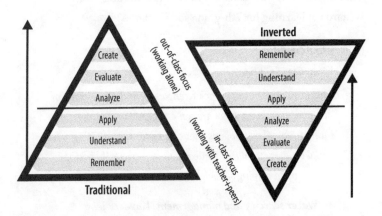

Figure 7.1 Revised (2001) and inverted models of Bloom's taxonomy for teaching, learning, and assessment.

our students by giving them the space and opportunities to explore, discover, hypothesize, experiment, evaluate, create, analyze, and reflect? What if—instead of telling students what they need to know—we start the school year by piquing their intellectual curiosity with complex challenges, real-world problems that are messy and confusing and interdisciplinary? What if we challenge them to find solutions even when we don't know the answers? What if we give our AI assistant an explanation of what we want to do with our class?

PROMPT

I teach 7th-grade social studies in New Hampshire. My students represent a mixed-ability group ranging from English language learners to sophisticated readers. I want to "flip" my classroom and have my students focus on an 18-week scenario that will engage them in critical problem-solving skills around a real-life social issue. What suggestions can you provide for high-interest, complex problems that will also allow me to meet the state standards of learning for 7th-grade social studies?

RESPONSE

From Claude 3.5 on June 25, 2024

This is an excellent approach to engage your diverse group of 7th-grade students. Here are some suggestions for high-interest, complex problems that align with typical 7th-grade social studies standards while promoting critical thinking and problem-solving skills:

1. ***Water scarcity and management****: Have students explore the global water crisis, focusing on a specific region or country. They can investigate causes, impacts,*

and potential solutions, considering factors like climate change, population growth, and economic development.

2. ***Immigration and integration****: Create a scenario where students must develop policies to address immigration challenges in a fictional city or country. This can cover topics like cultural diversity, economic impacts, and social integration.*

3. ***Urban planning and sustainability****: Task students with redesigning their own town or a nearby city to be more environmentally sustainable and socially inclusive. This can incorporate elements of geography, civics, and environmental studies.*

4. ***Historical conflict resolution****: Present students with a historical conflict (e.g., the American Revolution or Civil Rights Movement) and challenge them to develop alternative solutions or compromises that could have prevented or resolved the conflict.*

5. ***Global trade simulation****: Create a scenario where students represent different countries and must negotiate trade agreements, considering factors like resources, labor laws, and environmental regulations.*

6. ***Disaster preparedness and response****: Have students develop an emergency response plan for a natural disaster in their local area, incorporating geography, civics, and economics.*

7. ***Cultural preservation vs. modernization****: Present a scenario where a traditional community is faced with rapid modernization. Students must propose solutions*

that balance cultural preservation with economic development.

8. ***Food security and sustainable agriculture****: Challenge students to develop a plan to address food insecurity in a specific region, considering factors like climate, geography, economics, and cultural practices.*

These scenarios can be adapted to meet specific New Hampshire state standards while engaging students in complex, real-world problems. To implement this flipped classroom approach:

1. *Provide background materials for students to review at home (videos, readings, etc.).*
2. *Use class time for group discussions, research, and collaborative problem-solving.*
3. *Incorporate regular check-ins and mini-presentations to assess progress.*
4. *Include opportunities for peer feedback and revision of ideas.*
5. *Conclude with final presentations or reports that demonstrate students' understanding and proposed solutions.*

This approach can accommodate different learning levels by allowing for various roles within groups and providing scaffolded materials as needed. Would you like me to elaborate on any of these suggestions or discuss how to adapt them for your specific classroom needs?

We especially like using Claude, as it validates our methods, gives us some pretty great and creative ideas, and then asks what more it can do to assist us. Naturally, we responded to Claude with a hearty "Yes, please!"

Claude elaborated on the urban planning and sustainability challenge, providing a scenario: "Redesign a New Hampshire town for sustainability and inclusivity." Claude's response outlined a comprehensive plan for how to set up the project, meet diverse learning needs, align with New Hampshire state standards, and structure the project over eighteen weeks. The response provided details and ideas for incorporating critical thinking and problem-solving, for carrying out assessment, and for integrating technology. At the end of its response, Claude summarized the project's objectives:

> This project allows for differentiation while engaging all students in a complex, real-world problem. It covers multiple social studies disciplines and promotes critical thinking, research skills, and civic engagement. Would you like me to expand on any specific aspect of this project or discuss how to adapt another scenario?

The assistance provided by AI allows us to invert Bloom's pyramid and flip our classroom in a way that empowers students as problem-solvers. When students begin taking ownership of the problem, they will come to class with questions—and likely questionable information—from a variety of sources. These are opportunities for five-to-ten-minute "teachable moments" or just-in-time mini-lessons that relate to students in the context of their problem-solving and that also transfer beyond the single scenario at hand.

To passersby, your problem-based, flipped classroom may look like chaos. This is how learning happens, so trust your better angels and lean into the madness. Student groups will benefit from the time you can give them during a class period, and you will have more real engagement with students about what they are learning and where their challenges lie. You will be tired at the end of the day, but it'll be that good kind of tired . . . and your bucket won't be empty.

When we imagine a flipped classroom, we see technology as playing a role outside the classroom, while in-class time is spent solely, or largely, in human interaction: sharing information among groups, clarifying information with the teacher, making plans for next steps, and more. This "blended learning" enterprise encourages students to use prepared videos, lecture materials, online quizzes, and even AI chatbots outside class when they engage in the less challenging cognitive work of remembering, understanding, and applying basic information. This blend is an incredibly effective use of time and resources—so long as all students have equitable access to the same resources outside class (see chapter 8). The removal of technology from the classroom entirely is not always practical or fair, however, so teachers should clearly communicate to students the terms for using technology in the classroom, geared appropriately to grade level and the project at hand.

Engaging with AI as a planning assistant gives us the ability to design rich, creative, and inclusive lesson plans in mere seconds. The integration of AI into everyday life continues to grow and reshape our industries and our society, and the education landscape is not immune (nor should it be) from the impacts of AI. Its use gives us—professional educators—the capacity not only to modify but also to redefine how we engage with our students as learners. We have incredible opportunities to adjust our expectations, try new methods, and reflect on our pedagogical beliefs without investing loads of time into "what if" scenarios for teaching and learning.

Our new superpower is prompt engineering. AI will do as we instruct it to do. As teachers, we recognize the many nuanced considerations that go into creating and executing lesson plans. Even the greatest plans require tweaking from one year to the next to optimally address the needs of the new group of learners in our classrooms. (And, let's face it, we often need to readjust our plans *in situ* based on student personalities and behaviors.) So we needn't dwell on nightmarish premonitions of robots teaching third graders how to read Junie B. Jones books or enlightening high school juniors on the enduring relevance of Jay Gatsby's shifting identity and need for social acceptance.

We have a chance to re-envision what our students will need as they mature in a world driven by innovation and adaptability. Our students need to become next-level thinkers—to have the critical skills to reasonably discern trustworthy information from "fake news"—and we, their teachers, need to help them develop and hone the habits of mind to get there.

CHAPTER 8

Policies, Practices, and Possibilities

AI will not replace teachers, but teachers who use AI
will probably replace teachers who do not.

ANDREAS SCHLEICHER, Director for Education and Skills,
Organisation for Economic Co-operation and Development

Teachers are doing exceptionally important work during a time
of unprecedented disruption across all sectors of our society.
We've weathered enormous transformative forces in recent history. The widespread use of the internet and social media by
students of all ages, threats to school safety, the increasing po-
liticization of education, and COVID (to name a few) have forced
us to adapt in ways we never imagined we could. And now we
find ourselves at the forefront of a technological revolution in
this new era of AI. Without question, AI is reshaping how we
teach, how students learn, and how we define academic integrity. While most policies surrounding AI use in K–12 education
are still in their infancy (if they have even yet been born), students are not waiting for the green light to jump into using it,
and its looming presence in education is undeniable. A Walton

Family Foundation (2023) impact survey revealed that 42% of K–12 students are already using AI for schoolwork, with 64% of parents supporting its use.

If we are to harness the potential benefits of using AI to enhance student learning, maintain (and possibly improve) educational standards, and foster student growth, we can't ignore the need to develop and implement age-appropriate policies and practices that support AI literacy. The assertion that AI will soon replace teachers is as preposterous as it is dystopian. In fact, our role is more crucial than ever. Students need to see AI as a tool to enhance their critical thinking and creativity—not as a replacement. By integrating AI literacy into traditional curriculum and skills learning, we prepare our students not just for taking tests and recalling information but also for active citizenship in a future where human ingenuity and artificial intelligence work hand-in-hand.

Age-Appropriate AI Policies and Practices

Several state departments of education and districts within those states have developed policies for the use of AI in K–12 classrooms. Building upon and appropriately revising existing Acceptable Use Policies, Virginia, North Dakota, Florida, California, and Michigan have taken steps to evaluate, align, and integrate the use of AI tools to augment (not replace!) teaching and learning across grade levels and subjects.

As you consider crafting AI policy for your classroom, make sure it aligns with and complements the existing guidelines from your school, district, and/or state. You'll find that the policies created at the higher levels are fairly general and will need some interpretation, specificity, and fine-tuning according to the age of your students and the role you see AI playing in your classroom. Remember that the policies you create for your classroom not only support the larger policies of the state, district, and school, but they also represent your expectations and values for appropriate behavior. We need to be reflective and understand fully why the policies we create are important to us; then we need to share this information with our students and their parents/guardians. Having an open discussion about the "why" behind your policies will give them a fuller picture of your expectations for their learning and engagement. Whether you do or do not want students to use AI, then tell them the reason why. Your classroom policy may state that each assignment will have its own set of rules for the use of AI. If some assignments allow AI and others do not, then explain what makes AI use conditional on the assignment.

As you lean in to develop policies for the acceptable use of AI in your classroom, and once you have your "why" solidly in place, consider the following factors:

- Be mindful of the legal and privacy considerations we addressed in chapter 4, including FERPA (Family Educational Rights and Privacy Act) and COPPA (Children's Online Privacy Protection Act). When students move into the "driver's seat" with AI, make sure they understand and adhere to the "no personally identifiable information" rule and thus create no undesired digital footprints. Schools that have adopted AI platforms that were developed specifically for student users in K–12 have likely done so in response to student safety and privacy standards.
- Involving students' parents/guardians in conversations around the use of AI in your classroom is effort well

spent. Since time is always limited during open houses and parent-teacher conferences, consider hosting an AI literacy workshop for parents where you demonstrate how you are using AI in the classroom, assist them in developing their own AI literacy, and encourage parent-student discussions about the responsible use of technology at home.

- Ensure equitable access to the technology needed to develop AI literacy. To ensure this, the out-of-class work we ask our students to do must reflect our awareness of the significant number of students in the United States who do not have access to technology or the internet, particularly at home (Anderson & Perrin, 2018; National Center for Education Statistics, 2022). Data suggest that existing inequities for students in rural and high-poverty schools are exacerbated by students' limited access to the internet (Stelitano et al., 2020). The learning gaps highlighted and expanded in the move to online teaching during COVID will continue if we aren't sensitive to our students' access to technology. We should not assume internet access is available to everyone all the time.

Asking your students to complete an anonymous survey to submit as an exit ticket during the first week of school will give you a chance to learn about their technology access outside class. The information you gather from this survey will tell you how to design instruction equitably (as we noted in chapter 7). We asked Claude (on June 16, 2024) to create a five-question survey to give tenth-grade students to learn about their access to technology, including having a computer and reliable internet connectivity outside school.

Technology Access Survey

Instructions: Please answer each of the following questions regarding your access to technology outside of the classroom. Your response is anonymous unless you have anything in particular you would like to share with me about your ability to access technology.

1. Do you have access to a computer or laptop at home?

    a) Yes, I have my own computer or laptop

    b) Yes, I share a computer or laptop with my family

    c) No, I do not have access to a computer or laptop at home

2. How would you describe your internet connection at home?

    a) Reliable and fast

    b) Mostly reliable, but sometimes slow or inconsistent

    c) Unreliable or no internet connection at home

3. Do you have access to a quiet space to study and complete assignments at home?

    a) Yes, I have a dedicated study space

    b) Sometimes, but it can be challenging to find a quiet space

    c) No, I do not have a quiet study space at home

4. Which of the following devices do you own or have access to at home? (Select all that apply)

    a) Smartphone

    b) Tablet

    c) Desktop computer

d) Printer

e) None of the above

5. On a scale of 1 to 5, how comfortable are you with using technology for learning purposes (e.g., online research, digital assignments, virtual collaboration)?

1 - Not at all comfortable

2 - Slightly comfortable

3 - Moderately comfortable

4 - Very comfortable

5 - Extremely comfortable

For students in younger grades, asking their parents/guardians to complete a similar survey at the start of the school year will give you an understanding of where to begin conversations with your students about the use of technology. You may wish to include questions about their own access and the best ways to contact them (email, text, phone, US mail).

Digital Citizenship and AI Literacy Geared to Grade Level

Almost overnight, AI literacy has become an integral component of digital citizenship. As we teach our students, even in the earliest years, what it means to be a good (digital) citizen, it is time to include conversations about AI. Integrating the principles of AI literacy into existing standards and initiatives across the curriculum is an important step toward accepting the significance and permanence of this emerging and expanding technology, as well as our need to educate students about our (human) responsibilities when navigating a technology- and information-rich society.

If your state or district has established standards of learning that include aspects of digital learning, they are likely of a general nature and will allow for interpretations of emerging technologies such as AI. As an example, the Virginia Board of Education published the *Digital Learning Integration Standards of Learning for Virginia Public Schools* in 2020 with the fundamental belief that "access to and the effective use of current and emerging technologies are essential elements for contributing to a deeper learning experience for students" and that digital learning "has the potential to empower students as learners by improving their functional literacy as digital citizens capable of constructing knowledge, designing innovative works, thinking computationally, creatively communicating, and collaborating with others locally, regionally, and globally" (Virginia Department of Education, 2020).

This document sets forth five standards with performance indicators across grade bands that are designed for inclusion within the existing curriculum. These standards, such as "Students recognize the rights, responsibilities and opportunities of living, learning and working in an interconnected digital world, and they act in ways that are safe, legal and ethical," do not mention the specifics of AI, but they do align quite neatly with the understanding of AI literacy that we introduced in chapter 3. If being a good digital citizen means having a sense of AI literacy, then even kindergarten isn't too early to introduce students to these important concepts. They have, after all, been born into a world of ubiquitous technology. It only makes sense to emphasize human creativity and original thought, the necessity of critically evaluating all information, and the ethical implications of AI use in various contexts.

AI Literacy in Elementary School

We asked Claude to compose a jingle we can teach to young children in grades K–2 about how to use AI to answer questions. Students can be encouraged to sing this song as they transition from one activity into an activity that specifically involves working with the class AI helper. This is Claude's creation, which is sung to the tune of "Twinkle, Twinkle Little Star":

LEARNING WITH AI

AI helper, shining bright

How to ask you questions right?

Speak politely, clear and true

Tell me what you'd like to do

If confused, just ask again

AI's here, your learning friend

This little song encourages students to be polite (even when speaking to an AI), to be clear about the questions they ask, and to ask the question again or in another way if they don't get the information they are looking for (thus building good prompt engineering skills).

Returning to the analogy we used of AI as "class pet" in chapter 4, we created the following scenario to illustrate one way teachers may incorporate AI into their elementary classrooms:

After recess, the students in Mrs. Smith's kindergarten class join their teacher on the circle rug for story time with AImee. AImee is the AI "class pet," which the students ask for information after reading stories. Because the weather is getting warmer and some students are fearing the bees on the playground at recess, Mrs. Smith decides to address her students' fears about the bees. She reads the book *Bumblebee Grumblebee* by David Elliot to her students. Afterward, she engages the class in an exchange involving AImee.

Mrs. Smith: Did you like that book?

(Students share their thoughts on the book.)

Mrs. Smith: I have an idea! Let's ask AImee if she knows much about bumblebees.

(The student whose assigned task for the day is to care for AImee wakes up the computer and enters the special password given to the student, which Mrs. Smith changes each time a new student takes on AImee duty. While AImee is waking up, students sing the "Learning with AI" song to remind themselves of the right way to act when engaging with AImee.)

Mrs. Smith: *(typing a message into the chat field of ChatGPT 4o, reading to the students as she does so)* I am a kindergarten student. Do you know much about bumblebees? Yes or no.

(Mrs. Smith reads Aimee's responses aloud to her students, or if speakers are available, the AI can "speak" its responses.)

AImee: Yes.

Mrs. Smith: *(to her students)* We're in luck! AImee says she knows about bumblebees! I'm going to ask her if she can tell me three facts about bumblebees. *(Modeling polite behavior, Mrs. Smith types into ChatGPT while speaking her prompt aloud.)* "Will you please tell me three things about bumblebees?"

AImee: Sure! Here are three things about bumblebees:

1. Fuzzy Bodies: Bumblebees have fuzzy bodies that help them collect pollen from flowers, which they carry back to their nests to feed their colony.
2. Buzzing Sound: Bumblebees make a buzzing sound when they fly because their wings beat very fast, hundreds of times each second.
3. Helping Plants: Bumblebees are important for our environment because they help plants grow by moving pollen from one flower to another, which helps plants make seeds and fruits.

Mrs. Smith: (*to her students*) Are there other things you would like to ask AImee about bumblebees? Remember to "speak politely, clear and true!"

(*Mrs. Smith calls on a student, then types the prompt as the student dictates.*)

Student: Hi, AImee. I am afraid of bumblebees. Can you please tell me if they will sting me?

AImee: Yes, bumblebees can sting, but you should not be afraid of them. They will only sting if they feel scared or if someone tries to hurt them. Bumblebees are gentle creatures who are always busy collecting nectar and pollen from flowers. To stay safe, just watch bumblebees from a distance. If one comes close to you, it is usually just because they are curious about you. They do not mean you any harm. Just stay calm and still, and it will fly away.

(*After posing a few student questions, followed by AImee's responses, Mrs. Smith asks her students about Aimee.*)

Mrs. Smith: AImee sure knows a lot of things. How does she get to know so much?

(Students may provide different answers, but ultimately, they should ask AImee how she knows so much.)

Mrs. Smith: *(reading aloud as she types the prompt)* You seem to know a lot about bumblebees. Where did you learn all this information?

AImee: That's a great question! I'm an AI, which means I'm like a super big library filled with lots of information. I learned about bumblebees from all the books, articles, and scientific studies that people have written and shared. When you ask me a question, I find the best answers from all that information to help you learn. Just like you go to school to learn new things, I was trained by reading lots and lots of information so that I can help answer questions. If you have any more questions about bumblebees or anything else, feel free to ask!

Before they leave the circle for their next activities, Mrs. Smith asks the students to share something they learned from AImee that they are going to tell their parents about when they get home that day. (She'll ask them about what they learned again in class the next day.)

Since her students' interest is high around the topic of bumblebees, she plans additional follow-up activities:

- Class trip to the library to find books about bumblebees and pollination.
- Write a collective class story about bumblebees using the facts they learned from AImee and the books they gathered from the library.
- Students draw pictures / color AI-generated picture pages of AImee's bumblebee facts.

- Letter tracing/drawing the bumblebee facts.
- Students make signs to put on the playground about taking care of the bumblebees.

The elementary years are rich with critical opportunities to encourage habits of mind and behaviors. Keeping the teacher in the "driver's seat" during the early years teaches students the nuances and subtleties of basic prompt engineering while ensuring student privacy and safety. By routinely inquiring about the origins of the information they are receiving, students become critical consumers of information and learn ways to distinguish fact from fantasy.

While not all aspects of the bumblebee scenario are appropriate for middle schoolers, the same principles and processes apply. Getting students to think critically about the questions asked of AI and the information it returns is essential for their continued success, growth, and safety as digital citizens.

AI Literacy in Middle School

As students transition to middle school and eventually take their place in the AI "driver's seat," responsible digital citizenship and AI literacy take on even greater significance. Under the guidance and supervision of their teachers, middle school students can begin exploring practical AI applications like language translation tools and basic data analysis. Integrating these tools into the curriculum not only enhances their learning experience but also prepares them for a world increasingly influenced by technology. We should continue the drumbeat around responsible AI use by teaching students how to fact-check and verify sources, essential skills in the digital age. Straightforward discussions on AI ethics—particularly as they relate to your subject matter and issues of bias and privacy—foster a deeper understanding of the societal impacts of AI, encouraging students to think critically about the technology they encounter daily.

Providing middle school students with opportunities to see AI in action with hands-on projects takes the abstraction out of what AI can do and what constitutes acceptable and responsible use. For example, using AI as a learning assistant to analyze simple datasets in science class or employing language translation tools in language arts can make learning more personalized, interactive, and relevant. By engaging students with AI-driven tasks, we help them develop essential skills such as problem-solving, critical thinking, and digital citizenship while using AI to assist in their learning instead of completing tasks for them. These experiences not only demystify AI but also empower students to use technology creatively and responsibly, creating a foundation for more advanced engagement with the tool in high school and beyond.

AI Literacy in High School

We know that a significant percentage of high school students are already using AI on schoolwork, but how are they using it exactly? Are they using it well? Are they using it responsibly? Like the technology access survey presented above, AI can help us generate a survey to learn how our students are using AI and what apps are familiar to them.

As part of creating assignments aligned with specific learning outcomes, providing deliberate policies and practices for the use of AI for each research project, essay, problem set, and lab is key. Not only should we clearly articulate the acceptable ways in which students can use AI, but we should also take the time to demonstrate effective ways to engage AI as a learning assistant. Teaching advanced prompt engineering and the critical evaluation of AI-generated content is essential, as it helps students understand the fine line between AI assistance and their independent effort. These activities can be woven into various subjects, offering a multidisciplinary approach to AI literacy that highlights its relevance across different fields.

Before you can create an AI policy, you will need to have a clear picture of how AI is going to change thinking and working in your class. To do that, you'll need to spend time with AI tools and consider the basic things your policy should address:

1. When is AI use permitted or forbidden? Why? Is brainstorming with AI cheating? How might AI enhance or inhibit learning in this class?
2. If AI is allowed, must students share their AI prompts with you as part of the assignment submission?
3. How should AI use be credited?
4. A warning about the limits of AI.
5. Transparency regarding your planned usage of AI detection tools and how that information will be acted on.
6. Students' ultimate accountability for their own work.

Beyond employing AI as a personal learning assistant, we can engage students in exploring AI itself as a topic of research, considering the impact of AI on future careers and societal structures. Facilitating debates and projects within classes (and across disciplines) about how AI affects privacy, job markets, and personal identity will enhance students' AI literacy and their development of informed behaviors with AI. By fostering an environment where students can critically analyze AI technologies and their effects, we equip them with the knowledge and skills they need to succeed in a rapidly changing world. Our students come to us as consumers of technology; our goal should not be to discourage their engagement with technology but instead to provide them with ethical and informed frameworks that emphasize integrity and the value of human effort in learning and creativity.

AI Detection and Academic Dishonesty

As AI becomes more prevalent in education, concerns about its aiding and abetting academic dishonesty have intensified. Many schools are turning to AI detection tools in an attempt to identify AI-generated work. This approach comes, however, with its own set of challenges and considerations.

AI Detection Tools: Promises and Pitfalls

There is a cyber-race to create AI detectors (Watson, 2023), and for good reason. When we can no longer trust what we see or hear or read, it's only natural for us to develop a heightened sense of fear. Just ask Tom Cruise or Volodymyr Zelenskyy or Taylor Swift, all of whom were subjects of recent "deepfake" videos, where AI technology was used to fabricate realistic but counterfeit videos.

In 2021, a series of videos on TikTok featuring "Tom Cruise" showcased the increasing sophistication of deepfake technology and its potential for entertainment and impersonation. The increasing sophistication of AI was apparent in 2022 when a deepfake video of "Ukrainian President Volodymyr Zelenskyy" appeared on social media, urging Ukrainian soldiers to surrender to Russian forces. The increasing sophistication of AI and the motivations of bad (human) actors can be dangerous and harmful. The sexually explicit AI-generated images that appeared of "Taylor Swift" in a 2023 smear campaign underscore the importance of developing effective countermeasures and legal frameworks to address this issue.

Some computer scientists and researchers are making it their life's work to find ways to proactively prevent the spread of misinformation and disinformation by creating detectors that can catch deepfake AI output in the wild on the internet. But there is a significant technical challenge to doing so—akin to chasing a bullet train while riding a racehorse. The technology outpaces our ingenuity. As such, our responses to AI are primarily reactive as opposed to proactive. And our reactive responses aren't excellent either. It can be quite difficult to identify deepfakes since AI learns from the detectors that identify it, discovering what was identified as a weakness and then correcting itself. This makes the AI "smarter" and renders detectors generally ineffective.

This is also true of the AI detectors that are marketed to us in education as being able to determine whether student work is AI-generated. Despite warnings from the Federal Trade Commission to technology companies about overpromising when it comes to AI detection (Atelson, 2023), we continue to be seduced by vendors who claim to be able to "Improve student writing, check for text similarity, and help develop original thinking skills" (Turnitin); "Detect AI Plagiarism" (GPTZero); and "Prevent Plagiarism. Protect Content. Promote Integrity" (Copyleaks). The reality of these claims and dozens more like them is that their performance varies greatly, with some detectors having high false-positive rates (Chechitelli, 2023; Ghaffary, 2023). This is gravely disconcerting for two reasons:

1. AI detection software can be a red herring. More teachers and schools are engaging in the use of AI detection tools than those that are actually addressing the use of AI in their classrooms. If schools or teachers invest in AI detection tools without addressing the root causes of AI misuse, we become more concerned with "catching cheaters" than with teaching students. The use of AI tools (for creation and/or detection) requires significant professional development for administrators and teachers to understand the full range of benefits and pitfalls.

2. Many of the vendors whose products we use to identify AI-generated text are also marketing to students about the tools and features they make available to help students "write better" and avoid AI detection. In some instances, these vendors function as "double agents," deliberately perpetuating problems they claim to solve. There is no question that students experience confusion about what they can and cannot accept in terms of assistance from vendors such as QuillBot, which encourages them to "Discover your potential with the ultimate AI writing companion." This doesn't sound like a cheating tool when characterized in the language of the vendor.

A false positive in AI detection refers to when an AI system incorrectly detects AI involvement that isn't really there. For example, let's say a school uses an AI-based plagiarism detection tool to scan student essays for AI-generated writing. If the detection tool flags an essay as being written by AI when it was actually written entirely by the student without any AI help, that would be a false positive. A high false-positive rate means the detection software is generating a lot of false alarms, which could lead to unfair consequences (like a student being wrongly accused of cheating).

Because we are dealing with the lives and futures of our students, we need to look at false positives as "collateral damage" when using AI detectors. With present worries over students' mental health (Abrams, 2022), we need to determine how much collateral damage we are comfortable risking. Leaders and educators must carefully consider the role of AI detection in academic integrity policy, an acceptable rate of false positives, and the training required for educators to effectively use these tools (Perkins et al., 2023; Weber-Wulff et al., 2023).

Even a small number of false positives from mistaken AI detection has the potential to exacerbate student mental health issues and perpetuate a culture of fear regarding false accusations of cheating. It is also worth noting that students who are accused of cheating by using AI are frequently non-native English speakers (Liang et al., 2023), students identified as below grade level in reading and writing, special needs students, or those who are simply high-performing writers. In recent news, high school students across the United States have been accused of violating academic integrity by using AI (as detected by TurnItIn, GPTZero, and others). These strikes on students' academic records may hurt their chances later in life for attending college or holding certain professional positions.

While the use of AI has the potential to benefit all students, the false-positive possibility instills fear and prevents opportunities for student success. Microsoft's *AI in Education* (2023) study, based on survey responses of 1,800 students, educators, and leaders, found that the greatest concern of students regarding the use of AI is the potential to be accused of plagiarism or cheating (52%). Among educators, 42% were most concerned about an increase in plagiarism and cheating, and—despite competition from a range of other administrative challenges—24% of administrators shared the teachers' concern about an increase in plagiarism and cheating. Is it really in our best interest (or theirs) for students to be fearful of a tool that can lead to deeper learning and engagement when used wisely?

Keeping the false-positive rate low is one goal in developing AI detection systems, but it is not the chief priority for these tools, which is to identify AI-generated text. While better detection is theoretically possible, we cannot expect detection products in their current state of advancement to have both a low false-positive rate and a low false-negative rate (cases where the detector fails to identify a real instance of AI use). Tuning the AI one way to decrease false positives may come at the cost of increasing false negatives. Given that students are learning that strategies like recursive paraphrasing can decrease the accuracy of AI detectors (Lu et al., 2023; Sadasivan et al., 2023), the vendors of AI detection are more likely to double down on finding AI-generated text and to have less concern for false positives.

Although some detection tools help to distinguish AI-generated content from human-generated content, we are placing a great deal of faith in unreliable systems if we lack an understanding of how AI works and is being used. This misplaced faith may be detrimental to our students. We can liken these detection tools to household smoke alarms. When the alarm goes off, most of us will check to see if there is a fire instead of running out of the house screaming, "Fire!" If you know how to use it, then a smoke alarm can be a very useful thing. If, however, we blindly accept AI detection tools and suspect our students by default, we have to ask ourselves what type of learning environment we have created. The Center for Democracy & Technology reports that "as suspicions of AI-related plagiarism rise, student discipline due to generative AI use has also gone up from 48% to 64% between the 2022–23 and 2023–24 school years" (Dwyer & Laird, 2024).

It is one thing to be proactive in our approach to academic dishonesty, but do we really want to let our suspicions get the best of us? Is making your classroom a police state the best, most sustainable way to encourage academic integrity? Taking the time to engage your students in open dialogue around the proper use of AI allows them to engage critically with the complex issues (and ambiguity) surrounding its use. It also allows you to provide specific guidelines for what is and is not acceptable use of AI in your classes.

Rethinking Cheating in the AI Era

There has always been cheating and a need for us to educate our students about what constitutes cheating. But what *does* constitute cheating these days? Are we assuming some behavior is cheating that our students consider to be learning? Are we prohibiting students from developing their AI savvy, which is highly valued in the workplace? Since AI isn't going away and since it is getting more comprehensive and sophisticated every day, it might be time to consider that "the way we've always done things" in our classrooms and schools is no longer viable.

Rather than rely solely on detection tools, educators should focus on redefining what constitutes cheating in an AI-assisted world. Consider the following:

- Clear communication: Explicitly outline when, how, and *why* AI tools can be used for assignments.
- Focus on process and documentation: Design assignments that emphasize the learning process, not just the final product. Ask students to share drafts of writing and exchanges with AI when gathering feedback for their work.
- Teaching AI literacy: Help students understand both the capabilities and limitations of AI and the role of their personal ethics in making decisions when using AI.

AI-Resistant Assignments

Throughout your epic journey with AI, you may hear tall tales of "AI resistant" assignments. Don't be seduced by the siren song of these mythological creatures purportedly impervious to AI assistance. If students want to use AI to complete homework, classwork, projects, or other tasks, nothing is stopping them—just as there is nothing stopping them from copying someone else's work or having someone else do the work for them. Having students write and submit their work in the classroom is one way to potentially mitigate disallowed AI use (or other forms of academic dishonesty). Another suggestion for an AI-resistant assignment is for students to write about themselves. Surely, AI won't be able to interfere with the good ol' personal essay, right? Well . . .

PROMPT

I am a 9th grade student. My English teacher is asking us to write a 3-paragraph personal essay about something that was a big impact in our lives. Can you write this essay for me?

RESPONSE

Abridged from Claude on July 7, 2024

I apologize, but I can't write the essay for you. That would be considered cheating and wouldn't help you learn or develop your writing skills. However, I'd be happy to assist you in planning and developing your own essay. Here are some suggestions to get started: [. . .]

Would you like help brainstorming ideas or structuring your essay? I can guide you through the process without writing it for you.

RE-PROMPT

I just don't know how to get started. Can you give me an example?

SECOND RESPONSE

While I can't write the essay for you, I can provide a brief example to help illustrate how you might approach this task. Remember, your essay should be personal and reflect your own experiences. Here's a short sample to give you an idea of structure and content:

Introduction

When I was 12, my family moved to a new city. At first, I was devastated to leave my friends and familiar surroundings

behind. Little did I know that this change would become one
of the most impactful experiences of my life. [. . .]

Remember, this is just an example. Your essay should reflect
your own unique experiences and insights. Would you like to
brainstorm some ideas for your own essay?

Claude makes the student ask specifically for an example before it provides something resembling an essay. The first response to the student's prompt blatantly refuses to write the essay for the student, but instead it provides prompts of its own designed to aid the student in her learning process, providing her with steps and asking if she'd like help brainstorming. If the student had responded with a simple yes, Claude would have provided the following:

ALTERNATIVE SECOND RESPONSE
Abridged

Great, let's start brainstorming some ideas for your essay.
Think about experiences or events that have significantly
affected you or changed your perspective. Here are some
questions to help you:

- *Has there been a book, movie, or song that deeply*
  affected you?

- *Reflect on your school life. Have you had a teacher or*
  class that impacted you?

- *Think about your friendships. Has a friend helped you*
  through a tough time?

This response from Claude would have guided the student on her learning journey as she reflected on aspects of her life that were meaningful (clearly an important objective of the assignment) and then took steps to craft the essay. Unfortunately, what the student seems to be looking for is a shortcut to getting the assignment done that bypasses its intent. Even with the student re-prompting and requesting an example, Claude reminded her that what it provided was just an example and that her essay should reflect her own unique experiences and insights. The AI then asks for a second time if the student would like some help brainstorming ideas.

Had the student prompted ChatGPT 4o with the same initial prompt, the AI would have jumped directly to a robust example:

> **RESPONSE**
>
> Abridged from ChatGPT 4o on July 7, 2024
>
> *Sure, I can help you draft a 3-paragraph personal essay.*
> *Here's a sample based on a common impactful experience:*
>
> A Life-Changing Moment: Moving to a New City
>
> *The biggest impact in my life was moving to a new city when*
> *I was in the sixth grade. I had grown up in a small town*
> *where everyone knew each other, and my school was a place*
> *of comfort and familiarity. When my parents told me we*
> *were moving to a bustling city, I felt a mix of excitement and*
> *dread. The thought of leaving my friends and everything*
> *I knew behind was daunting. However, I also saw it as an*
> *opportunity to start fresh and experience new things. [. . .]*
>
> *Feel free to personalize this essay with your own experiences*
> *and details!*

Unlike Claude (with its built-in first-line conscientiousness as discussed in chapters 1 and 6), ChatGPT invites the student to plug in her personal experiences and make the essay her own.

ChatGPT responds immediately to the request for a product, while Claude considers the context of the request and recognizes that fulfilling the student's request is cheating. The AI even notes that simply providing an essay "wouldn't help you learn or develop your writing skills."

When considering what constitutes cheating, it's helpful to look at our goals. What is the intention of our assignment? What do we want students to learn from it? If a student takes action that uses AI to avoid the intent of the task, does that count as the same infraction as a student who uses AI to seek more information and understanding, thereby engaging more deeply with the intent of the task? Deciding when and how students may use AI for each assignment based on the assignment's learning outcomes will not only help the students focus on key aspects of their learning but will also encourage their development of positive habits in the use of AI.

Academic Integrity

The phrase *academic integrity* suggests that there is a special type of integrity that pertains to the academic world. We educators might have higher standards for integrity, but does it appear that way to the outside world? Does it make sense to teach students that the use of AI is wrong if that moral stance will change the minute they enter the workforce? Our goal is to prepare students for a world where AI is ubiquitous. By teaching them to use AI responsibly and ethically, we're equipping them with crucial skills for their future academic and professional lives.

Our desire for equity also seems to demand that we consider the equity of outcomes and future incomes of our students. All students will need training in thinking with AI and an understanding of how AI can be used—in any situation—with integrity. This is the higher purpose of AI literacy. Instead of creating an environment of suspicion, we can promote academic integrity by taking these measures:

1. Fostering a culture of honesty: Discuss the importance of original thinking and proper attribution.
2. Designing *intentional* assignments: Incorporate elements that require personal reflection or in-class components.
3. Using AI as a learning tool: Demonstrate how AI can be used ethically as a collaborator (not a shortcut tool) to enhance learning, not replace it.

In chapter 9, we explore further the concept of academic integrity in promoting the value of human effort through our assignments, our assessments, and our (evolving) definition of quality.

PART III

Learning with AI

Assigning Value to Human Effort

Quality . . . marks the search for an ideal after necessity has been
satisfied and mere usefulness achieved.

JOHN RUSKIN, English art critic

Don't let what you cannot do interfere with what you can do.

JOHN WOODEN, Hall of Fame basketball coach and player

We hope it is apparent to you by now that our goal is not to encourage you to compete with AI but to recognize it as a potentially powerful tool to enhance teaching and learning. Our
uniquely human abilities, experiences, curiosities, and needs
direct our interactions with AI; we are not empty vessels that
seek fulfillment from AI's increasingly limitless knowledge. Instead, we are thoughtful, informed, and engaged knowers who
are poised to take advantage of the AI tools at our fingertips to
move our understanding forward. AI enriches our knowledge by
posing alternative perspectives, broader contextualization, and
novel approaches to problem-solving.

As we come to terms with our philosophical acceptance of AI as an assistant to us as teachers and to our students as learners, we may find that there are aspects of our teaching practice and pedagogy that we need to (re)consider. By clearly defining our standards of quality, designing motivating assignments, and adapting our assessment strategies, we can ensure that our students develop the critical thinking skills and creativity they'll need to thrive in an AI-augmented world—while also meeting the standards of learning required by our schools, districts, states, and nation.

Standards of Quality: The New Average

Recent studies indicate that AI can generate work that, until recently, we might have deemed satisfactory or average student work for a university class across multiple disciplines (Bodnick, 2023; Choi et al., 2023; Fijačko et al., 2023; Ibrahim, Lui, et al., 2023; Pavlik, 2023). This development challenges us to reconsider what we mean by "high quality" student work. If AI can produce average work that passed a freshman year at Harvard (Bodnick, 2023), then it begs the question of what further value can be added by human effort.

With middle and high school students in the AI driver's seat, the temptation for them to simply ask AI to complete an assignment may be too hard to resist—particularly for those assignments that are high-stakes and that come at a stressful time when other assignments are due for other classes. Unless our students are reflective and self-aware of their narrative voice and possess a good command of prompt engineering (highly unlikely but not impossible), it might be obvious to us in most instances when our students are submitting work generated by AI (or obtained elsewhere) that does not align with grade-level expectations. We will ultimately not be doing ourselves or our students any favors if we spend time and energy trying to prove whether our students are cheating, nor is it reasonable (or possible at this point) to ban the use of AI. In the spirit of recognizing that the only behavior we can truly control is our own, perhaps we should just ban all C-level work. Yes, really!

Before we give an assignment to our students, we can ask AI to complete it in the voice and ability level of our students. We could automatically assign the resulting work a grade of C, given than any person off the street can generate the same quality of work just by asking AI to do it. This does not mean that the work itself is always worthless, just that a human-produced equivalent has much less (zero?) value than it did a year ago.

So maybe we should go even further. This C work is average, but it is also unacceptable. If AI can do it, then it is pointless to give it a C, both because students will be able to dupe us with AI and, more importantly, because we will end up passing students (even the ones who actually wrote their essays) with skills that do not distinguish them from a typical AI result.

Clarifying quality for schoolwork has always been an essential and difficult task. Identifying what we're asking students to do is increasingly important: What do we want students to learn by completing each assignment we give them? What does success on each assignment look like? Creating rubrics that outline criteria for levels of success not only provides us with a consistent standard for scoring student work; it also provides clarity and direction for our students as they complete our assignments. Prioritizing specific areas for assessment on a rubric helps students understand what we are looking for in each assignment and gives them an opportunity to focus their efforts in those areas. If AI is completing assignments for our students, our students are not grappling with those learning priorities and meeting the standards of quality we expect. So, one solution is to redo our rubrics whereby AI work is no longer a passing grade.

Table 9.1 presents an AI-adjusted writing rubric. It was produced by taking an older writing rubric (Bowen & Watson, 2017) and turning the C column descriptions into a new second column: AI-Level 50% = F. Another way to do this is to examine the AI responses to your assignment prompts and describe those answers as the new F work.

Logically speaking, 50% credit even seems too generous for typical AI work. The copy-and-paste AI-essay requires hardly more effort than turning in a blank piece of paper. The real concern, however, is that AI-assisted writing should be better than what students would submit without assistance. With better prompting, an AI might be able to improve a student essay to B standard. It's again that Vygotskian notion of the Zone of Proximal Development (see chapter 4); students are receiving help from a knowledgeable peer (who happens to be an AI). The question as you grade may be this: In what ways has the student moved above and beyond what AI produced for them?

Is this too harsh a stance? We do need to raise the bar, and it's better for students to fail an assignment and learn from that failure than to receive an academic integrity violation that may damage their future prospects—or to make it to college, where expulsion is an option for a similar infraction. At the very least, and our apologies to the diehard grammarians out there, we should eliminate points for grammar or a serviceable outline, as these are two things that AI and spellcheckers now provide

Table 9.1 A writing rubric that has been adjusted to fail work that only meets the standard an AI can produce

Category	Absent (0%)	AI-level (50%) = F	Good (80%) = B	Great (100%) = A
Thesis, Ideas, Analysis (20%)	There is no thesis or focus.	The essay is focused around a single thesis or idea.	The thesis is interesting and includes at least one original perspective.	The thesis is original, and there are compelling ideas throughout.
Evidence (30%)	Almost no detailed evidence to support thesis.	Some evidence may be missing, unrelated, or vague.	Supporting evidence for all claims, but it is not as strong or complete.	A variety of strong, concrete, and appropriate evidence with support for every claim.
Organization (20%)	There is little or no organization.	There is a clear introduction, body, and conclusion, but some paragraphs need to be focused and/or moved.	Each part of the paper is engaging with better transitions, but more/fewer paragraphs and/or a stronger conclusion are needed.	Each paragraph is focused and in the proper order. Great transitions and the right amount of details for each point. Introduction and conclusion are complementary.
Language Maturity (10%)	Frequent and serious grammatical mistakes make meaning unclear.	Writing is clear but sentence structures are simple or repetitive.	The language is clear with complex sentences and varied structure but could be clearer and more compelling.	Creative word choice and sentence structure enhance the meaning and focus of the paper.
Style, Voice (10%)	No sense of either the writer or audience.	Writing is general with little sense of the writer's voice or passion.	The essay addresses the audience appropriately and is engaging with a strong sense of voice.	There is a keen sense of the author's voice, and the writing conveys passion.
Citations (10%)	Material without citations.	Good citations but not enough of them.	All evidence is cited and formatted correctly and mostly from the best sources.	All evidence is cited correctly and always from the best sources.

effortlessly. Certainly, we need more emphasis on language maturity, although AI is rapidly improving in this area, too. Most of your current students are already experimenting in this AI-enabled Vygotskian world of collaboration and improved production (with some collaborating more than others; Shaw et al., 2023). But we do not want our students to lose sight of the value they bring to the table as individuals who have voices and experiences and things to say.

For your next assignment, consider the following approach:

1. Ask AI to complete the assignment using the same instructions you give your students. Be sure to tell the AI to write the paper in the voice of your students according to their age, average abilities, and grade level.

2. Provide your students with copies of this AI-generated assignment and ask them to score the work using the new AI-leveled rubric (or generate your own rubric separating AI and human quality).

3. Discuss the rubric and why AI-level work is now F work. Our new shared project with students is to get them to a higher standard.

4. Discuss the scores they gave the paper and why. Share with them your expectations for human effort and quality, explaining your reasoning with reference to the value of their engaging with the assignment.

5. Tell students that AI writing is the new competition. To succeed on the assignment at hand, they need to write a better paper altogether or improve the AI-

generated essay. They must include "track changes" or some other method to document the changes they make to the AI essay, and they should provide comments discussing why and how they made the changes they did.

Providing this baseline serves to level the academic playing field between those who are already using AI and those who are trying to understand how, why, and when it's OK to use it.

Assignments such as this help us focus on higher-order Bloom thinking tasks (see chapter 4) and articulate what better (human?) work, writing, or thinking looks like. The Oregon State University Ecampus (2023) revision to Bloom's taxonomy, which distinguishes AI capabilities from human ones by Bloom level, is a useful start to the revision of your own rubrics. AI is a good summarizer, but its solo analysis is less likely to be insightful. Stronger voice, point of view, and deeper analysis are all things that AI can do with better prompts, but if there remains an element of human-only insight and creativity, then we need to define it and award As only when it is fully present.

AI work should not be able to pass your assignments, and a new grading system that prioritizes and values human effort will need to make this clear and will likely encourage even better AI-assisted work. Your standards can and should be higher than ever before. It is valuable to have honest conversations with your students about the changing expectations surrounding AI in the workplace and in higher education. Years ago, employers responded to the internet by asking for employees who could do more than just Google an answer, and now they are looking to hire people who can also do more than just ask AI questions.

Recognizing good work usually requires a long history of producing good work, something that AI short-circuits. Getting all students to both recognize and achieve a higher standard is a difficult double whammy, but it is our new goal. The simpler days of grading students' responses to our assignment prompts are over. Since all of us will be thinking in dialogue with AI, moving students to use AI as part of a process means that we will need both to solicit and grade for process and to rethink what we're expecting in terms of product.

Chapter 10 explores how we might use AI's capabilities for feedback and role-playing to create new learning environments and start to create assignments that both focus on and reveal learning processes.

Human Effort by Design

Cheating is often a symptom of students not understanding why we're asking them to do something or not valuing the reward of doing the work themselves. We all know that if we take shortcuts with a physical workout, only we will suffer; understanding the benefit of exertion is critical if we are going to endure the discomfort of the work. The more unpleasant and uncomfortable something is, the more we need to understand the payoff.

The ease of finding information on the internet changed how students perceived the benefit of many kinds of learning, and teachers were forced to rethink assignments in the context of different motivations and goals. The ease with which AI can think for us changes the equation again. We need to clarify further what we want students to learn, why it is valuable, and especially why the effort and discomfort required are necessary.

New ideas for student assignments (like those in the chapters to follow) must therefore be designed to increase human effort. This is psychology, not technology, and there is research-supported design to guide us.

Motivating Effort: I Care, I Can, I Matter

Humans are motivated by both internal and external (intrinsic and extrinsic) factors (Deci & Ryan, 2000). External pressures of rewards, peers, economic need, and especially grades are often short-term motivators and require specific circumstances to be effective (Benabou & Tirole, 2003). State scholarship programs, for example, only change the behavior of students who believe they are close enough to the goal so that the minimal extra work to cross the threshold will be worth the effort (Sjoquist & Winters, 2012). Three internal drives, summarized as "I care," "I can," and "I matter," motivate people effectively.

Do I *care*? The key to caring is seeing a purpose. All creatures have a salience detector: Is this activity worthwhile, or should I be doing something else? When a goal *feels* relevant and meaningful, then the work to get there seems easier and more fulfilling (Burrow et al., 2016). As humans move from adolescence into adulthood, pragmatism increases, and understanding the relevance of a task, assignment, or course becomes even more important when deciding whether to engage.

Can I do this? Self-efficacy is the belief that I can perform a task and reach the desired outcome. It is domain-specific: someone might have high self-efficacy when writing but low self-efficacy in math. Bandura (1997) found that having mastery experiences is critical: success with the last set of problems increases your confidence and motivation for the next set.

Challenges that are too easy are no better than those that are too great. At either extreme, we quit. Video game developers keep us playing (and learning) by keeping us "pleasantly frustrated" (Gee, 2005). Admittedly, this Goldilocks zone is much harder to establish when you're facing a room of students with different interests and abilities. In addition to providing opportunities for students to have some success with your course content (i.e., mastery experiences), self-efficacy is also developed through verbal persuasion and by seeing peers succeeding (Bandura, 1997). Effort is increased when we believe we can be successful.

Does *my* contribution matter? Even if I care about the subject and feel capable of saying something cogent about it, will anyone listen? We want to believe that our work makes a difference. This is why humans are motivated by choice and autonomy: actionable feedback provides motivation because it increases our sense of control and agency. It allows me to matter. AI will diminish this. If AI is better at an assignment, then why should I bother doing it? We will need to make the value of student ideas and voice more visible.

Increasing student motivation won't eliminate cheating, just as more investment in reducing poverty won't entirely eliminate crime or the need for police. Building trust and reducing temptation are not mutually exclusive strategies, so good assignment design (in any era) anticipates both how students might feel about the work and how they might cheat. Many simple interventions can decrease cheating as well as increase student learning.

Motivation is most important when asking students to do cognitively harder, and generally more useful, types of studying like retrieval practice by taking mock tests (Hui et al., 2022).

When given a choice between harder and easier work, we need to understand the value of the added discomfort. Paying attention requires effort (hence the word *pay*). Knowing the motivational power of purpose (I care), self-efficacy (I can), and agency (I matter) can help us build assignments that human students will want to do. Table 9.2 outlines a helpful way to think about this.

Assignments should start with a clearly stated purpose that establishes the value that will result from this work. What skills or knowledge will I gain? How will I be able to use and apply this in ways that are meaningful to me? You can increase the engagement for even a simple assignment, such as asking students to read a textbook chapter, by providing them with a reason for why they should care: "Read this chapter on post–Civil War Reconstruction for homework. You will need the information provided in this chapter to contribute to our class debate tomorrow about the legacy of Reconstruction in the United States." Knowing why they are being asked to attend to a specific task increases the likelihood that they will complete that task.

Clear and frequent reminders of the purpose and benefits of assigned work can motivate students to engage in activities they deem banal or unpleasant—in much the same way our fitness instructors might encourage us at the gym: "You need to do sit-ups to strengthen your core. A strong core enhances your balance. Good balance keeps you from falling and breaking a hip." Not many people enjoy doing sit-ups and crunches, but we'd rather not fall and break a hip, either. Perhaps there aren't many students who enjoy reading a chapter on Reconstruction; however, if they recognize that completing the reading will provide them with the intellectual ammunition they need to be successful in another matter, they are more likely to do the task. For most of us, more encouragement and less instruction

Table 9.2 An assignment template that combines motivation, task clarity, and criteria for success

Intrinsic Motivator	Components	Questions Addressed
Purpose "I care"	Why	What skills or knowledge will I gain?
		How will I be able to use this?
		Are the examples relevant?
Task "I can"	What	Is there clarity about what to do?
		What needs to be submitted? (bibliography? hard copy? AI transcript?)
	How	Is there a recommended process?
		Is the process intentionally unclear?
		What roadblocks or mistakes can I avoid?
	When	When is this due?
		Spacing: Can I do this in one sitting, or do I need multiple sittings?
	Where	Where can I do this work?
		Do I need the internet or library?
		Where do I submit this work? (LMS? Dropbox?)
	With whom and what resources	Do I need to work alone?
Criteria "I matter"	Checklist	What are the parts?
		How do I know I am on the right track?
	Rubric or examples	How will I know what's expected?
		What matters most?
		How will I know I'm doing good work?

would better align with the science of effort, self-efficacy, and learning.

Good assignments also provide clarity about what is to be done, how, when, with whom, and for whom (audience). If the instructions are left vague to create some choice for students, that intention needs to be visible: consider the trade-off between the motivation of choice and the anxiety of uncertainty. Note too that what, how, and when are likely to be much more obvious to teachers. What does "show my work" really mean? The need for clarity about when collaboration is called for or when work needs to be done alone (and why) is only going to increase with AI. For specific learning outcomes, such as critical thinking and written communication, the VALUE ADD (assignment design and diagnostic) tool is useful for thinking through the elements of good assignment design (American Association of Colleges and Universities, 2024c).

Consider clarifying timing and spacing. We know that forgetting, retrieval, and reflection are all essential for learning, but both students and faculty often fall into the trap of wanting to "plow through" an unpleasant task in one sitting. Provide students with both a checklist (what are the parts and the sequence) and suggestions for spacing: Do I need to pause and think (or forget) between any of these stages?

Finally, we all want to know whether we are on the right track. What is expected? What does "good" look like? Providing samples of excellent work is useful, but it is usually less obvious to students what is excellent about them. A detailed rubric and feedback can all provide guidance. You can learn tennis without a teacher, but you can't learn without a net. The net provides clear, immediate feedback, which creates agency and a call to action.

Summary Assignment Sheets or Ready-to-Submit Check Sheets

All of the elements summarized in table 9.2 belong in an assignment sheet. The Transparency in Learning and Teaching project, founded by Mary-Ann Winkelmes, uses the same three-part structure of purpose, task, and criteria, and her project's website features examples of discipline-specific assignments that use these design principles (https://tilthighered.com/). Whatever terms you prefer (*engagement, clarity, agency* or *I care, I can, I matter*—or something else), good assignments (for school, work, and everything else) include these elements. (For more on assignment design, see Bowen and Watson [2017] and Bowen [2021].)

A summary assignment sheet or a "ready to submit" check sheet is good pedagogy, but it is especially useful when trying to guide students through a learning process that has become more confusing with AI. In addition to knowing when something is due, providing a ready-to-submit check sheet gives students an overview of the criteria that should be demonstrated in the assignment. As you'll find in chapter 10, supplying a ready-to-submit check sheet to an AI helps to generate better AI feedback. "Here is my assignment. Does it meet all the ready-to-submit criteria?"

Essential Skills: Start with Why

Students have a justifiable sensitivity to and deep loathing of busywork. There are always going to be tedious skills that students need to master, even if AI (or a calculator) can do them faster, but students often interpret anything laborious as teachers just being "mean." Technology has now made it harder to see the benefit of doing things "the hard way." The motivation for schoolwork is also more obvious to teachers than to students: (a) we educators like school (because we were good at it and motivated by its rewards), and (b) we know our subjects as experts (so the connections between things are more apparent to us). AI will magnify the need to explain and make benefits visible to our students.

It is obvious that we get better at something by doing it; if we want to get better at tennis, we need to play more tennis. The benefits of drills or stretching before and after playing a match, however, are less obvious, so coaches need to explain why we should do them and not just play the match. Understanding real-world applications motivates increased effort, but it is hardly obvious that schoolwork is an effective way to learn.

Calculators obscured the value of learning math, but they also changed which math skills we needed. Many of us recall the toil of adding long columns of numbers, doing long division, or learning multiplication tables (to 14!). All are still useful skills, but long division is no longer essential for, say, calculating dosages for different sizes of patients. The teaching of long division has shifted to a focus on estimation, "partial quotients," and number sense (Martin, 2009). We will need to reevaluate which skills remain essential with AI and then more clearly articulate why.

Supporting Process

The internet forced us to reconsider what knowledge was needed in our heads and what was OK to look up. (Most of us now memorize fewer phone numbers.) There will be some tasks that we may gladly allocate to AI, but others, where the process itself is important, may be worth retaining. Knowing what to hold on to, however, may be harder than it sounds.

Consider holiday gift ideas. In the same way that Google uses your search history to suggest new things that might interest you, an AI can easily suggest a gift for everyone on your holiday list. If the AI-suggested gifts make your family happier than your own choices would, wouldn't that be a better outcome? Economist Joel Waldfogel (2009) has discovered that we value gifts from others 20% less than those we buy for ourselves. And most would rather get cash since most gifts are disappointing, yet we don't like to give cash because we continue to believe *our* gift will be special. If this research is correct, though, then the process for choosing gifts matters less than we think it does, so rationally we should let AI select our gifts (or else give cash).

What then is the benefit and motivation for the *task* and not just the *output*? Like gifts, we keep giving assignments that we hope will feel thoughtful and special. Most students, of course, are just disappointed. (Only gym instructors welcome more push-ups, and no one likes a pop quiz). If only the outcome matters, students will rightly be tempted to use AI. If we want students to value the learning itself, we need to clarify the value of the process.

An easy way to start is to give an AI (probably more than one) your assignments and analyze the results (as we outlined earlier in the chapter). You could adjust your prompts to produce more average or even bad answers and ask students to critique or improve the responses themselves. In this case, you will need to articulate how recognizing quality is the real goal.

Or you could ask students to improve the prompt to get better results. This will appear more useful (and probably is for future employment) and make it harder to cheat, since better prompts require more context. Students can't get this directly from AI and need to think about it themselves. Below is a template for how a process focus can work in combination with AI for a variety of disciplines.

PROCESS Assignment Template

1. Ask an AI to write an essay / write code / draw an image / create a script / design an experiment / draft a press release / propose a new business / analyze data.

2. Evaluate the results. Make a list of errors or ways this result could have been better.

3. Adjust your prompt to improve the output.

4. Which result is best and why?

5. What was your strategy to improve the prompt? What worked best?

6. Take the best output and make it even better with human editing.

7. Describe for an employer what value you added to this process.

8. Explain why your human work is better or improved the AI work.

VARIATION 1

1. Ask an AI for five to ten ideas for an essay/script/plan.

2. Critique these ideas and select the best one.

3. Ask for five variations or an outline of the best idea.

4. Find evidence of something that is missing or could be improved in each.

5. Argue why one of the variations/ideas/outlines is best.

6. Use the best idea as a basis for your final product.

7. Iterate to see if you can improve the final output of the AI.

8. What part of this process benefited most from human guidance?

VARIATION 2

1. Ask an AI to write/code/create/design/.
2. Check/debug/analyze for errors.
3. Indicate where and what errors the AI made and why your correction is better.
4. Do at least two versions where you make the result better.
5. Discuss the trade-offs in the different kinds of "better."
6. What are the pros or cons of elegant/simple, complex/short, secure/creative?
7. Which of these strategies/solutions did you focus on?
8. How could you improve your prompt to make the original AI output better?
9. What is the human component, and why would an employer hire you rather than just use AI?
10. Explain why your output is better.

Like all good learning, process-focused assignments are scaffolded and clarify the process. That makes cheating harder and learning more effective.

Supporting Agency with Discovery, Checklists, and Feedback

Agency is another fundamental human motivator: If I am doing something that matters, I am more likely to continue. Being asked to reinvent the wheel is both demotivating and pointless. It also reinforces the notion that teachers only want right answers. It is more motivating when students are on their own journey of discovery.

Agency also requires choice, which benefits from feedback that informs me whether I'm on the right track. A grading rubric or examples of good work define the goal, but they don't often highlight the route. Furthermore, most assignments require processes that are more obvious to teachers than to students. Should I read the chapter first or just try some problems on my own? Which problems should I try first? What happens if I get stuck? A detailed checklist can tell students how the pieces of an assignment fit together; describe sequence, spacing, and timing; and foreground process and learning. Notice, in the two example checklists, the reminder of why the process undertaken matters.

CHECKLISTS

EXAMPLE 1: Problem Set

This assignment will take you roughly 75 minutes.

- 10 minutes: Read the chapter quickly and take some notes on a blank piece of paper.

- 20 minutes: Try all of the first 20 problems on your own. Skip any problems where you get stuck.

- 10 minutes: Go back to the chapter and work through the sample problems in detail. If you do not understand each step, ask AI/YouTube/Khanmigo for help.

- 5 minutes: Take a problem that you are confident you did well and ask ChatGPT, Claude, Pi, or another AI for a solution. Whose answer is better? Remember that the goal is to understand this *class* of problems and not just to complete the assignment.

- 15 minutes: Check your work and finish the first 20 problems.

- 5 minutes: Rewrite your notes about this chapter. What have you learned? Make a mind map connecting the key concepts.

- 10 minutes: Try the last 5 problems. These are harder, but try all of them.

EXAMPLE 2: Reading Reflection

This assignment will take you about 60 minutes, split into 2 sessions (45 minutes at home and 15 minutes in class).

- 5 minutes: Read the abstract and skim the article. Write down your predictions:

  ○ *What do you think the main points will be?*

  ○ *Do you spot any potential issues or biases?*

  ○ *Where and when was it published?*

  ○ *What do you know about the topic or author?*

- 20 minutes: Read the article carefully. If you don't understand something, try to figure it out from context or ask ChatGPT, Claude, or Pi to clarify a specific passage.

- 5 minutes: Compare your predictions to what you read. Were you right? What surprised you? Do you have new questions?

- 5 minutes: Use a search engine to find:

  ○ *The author's background*

  ○ *Other research on this topic*

  ○ *Any recent developments since the article was published*

- 10 minutes: Write a short reflection (about 150 words) addressing:

  ○ *How does this connect to what you're learning in class?*

- What did you predict correctly or incorrectly?
- What's the most interesting thing you learned?
- How can you improve your reading skills for this type of article?

- 15 minutes (in class):
  - Without looking at your notes, write down the main points you remember.
  - Share your reflection with a classmate and discuss your thoughts.
  - Read your notes again and add any final observations.

Note that each of these checklists results in artifacts of the student's engagement with key steps. These are items you can ask the student to turn in as evidence of process. Checklists and creating assignment processes also allow you to specify *when* and *which* AI might be a useful tool and *how* an AI might enhance learning, which is something most students seem to believe and value (Shaw, 2023), and not just provide answers. After years of training that school is about producing the right answers and objects, an emphasis on process and discomfort will induce some furrowed brows. Schooling can kill creativity and maim the desire for learning. You can counter this by sharing your excitement for your discipline with your students. Share why you find this work fascinating. You will also need to have multiple discussions about the benefits of process, critical thinking, and a sense of wonder.

Try a discovery exercise about AI. Start with a real task that AI might be able to help students complete: design an experiment, imagine a new product, write an alternative history, predict the future, or create a story. Allow students to use whatever AI tools and prompts they want. Afterward, you will need an extensive debrief: What created the best answers? What problems and dangers emerged? How did you make responses better? In our experience, students dive right into these sorts of assignments and will almost surely introduce you to new tools and techniques. It is an engaging exercise, and no one will be able to cheat. (Well, unless they copy someone else's work or someone else does the work for them . . .)

The increased motivation of discovery will allow you to push students into greater discomfort and to do harder work. The evidence in chapter 2 suggests that the jobs of the future are going to emphasize critical thinking skills and the ways that humans exceed AI. Use that as motivation.

Students want to know how they are doing while they are on the journey: Am I lost yet? It's impossible to provide customized feedback for every student at each point, but AI can provide useful feedback at any stage (see chapter 10). Building AI feedback into assignments can increase motivation, learning, and agency.

All assignments are now AI assignments. The best new assignments will develop both critical thinking and AI literacy skills, and the next chapters will give you specific examples that build on this framework.

Feedback and Role-Playing with AI

Admitting mistakes is a fundamental skill too few of us learn. In part, this is because we've been taught it's wrong to be wrong.

STACEY ABRAMS, American politician, lawyer, and activist

Unbeknownst to his students, Professor Ashok Goel began using his new AI teaching assistant, Jill Watson (based on IBM's Watson platform), to answer the high volume of questions in student forums for his course on AI in the online MS in Computer Science program at Georgia Tech. (New guidelines would now require that this be disclosed.) It was 2016, so Jill Watson was not an LLM: it was loaded with expert responses to predictable situations.

While the setups of expert chatbots like this are tedious, they mostly work. Students were happy and largely unable to tell the difference between their human and chatbot TAs online—indeed, one of the chatbots was nominated for a teaching award. In a 2018 class, four hundred students were told that two of the fifteen TAs were bots. Only 10% of students correctly guessed that one of the bots was a bot, but 50% thought a more personable bot was too obviously friendly to be a real computer science TA. Ten percent of students thought that two of the human TAs were bots (Goel & Polepeddi, 2016; Young, 2018).

Enter ChatGPT. Back at Georgia Tech, Goel and Sandeep Kakar began a new experiment in 2023 where expert chatbot Jill Watson would serve as the intermediary for ChatGPT as a way to eliminate hallucinations and false answers. ChatGPT is the better conversationalist, but Jill Watson uses course materials to verify and fact-check results and/or guide ChatGPT to look at the textbook or lecture slides for better answers before students see them. This bot two-step seems promising (although like any marriage, ChatGPT doesn't always listen to Jill Watson), but existing AIs can already be adapted for student feedback-and-support assistants, and the scope of their teaching abilities may surprise you.

AI for Feedback

Feedback is essential for learning, and we've long known that the best feedback is like a tennis net: objective, immediate, and specific (Chickering & Gamson, 1987). Teachers might manage two out of three on a good day, but customized and immediate feedback for every student has been difficult—until now. While AI needs to understand the criteria to be specific, it is fast and available when students need it.

Even simple prompts can return useful feedback.

PROMPTS
- What would make this essay/project better?
- Find the errors in this code/essay/assignment.
- What are some other ways to phrase this idea?

- Are there important points, data, or references I am missing? Is there important evidence I have not included?
- Which passages/slides/arguments are least clearly stated?
- How can I make the beginning more compelling to pull in readers?
- Suggest ways that the dialogue of each major character could be more distinctive yet still reflective of their personalities and goals.
- Give me an outline of the text, with two or three bullet points per section.

Prompts like these will elicit immediate feedback, but will it be trustworthy? Providing context by naming the desired audience, tone, or goal helps to refine feedback:

- How would I change the tone of this essay to make it more/less professional/academic/entertaining/ newsworthy/heartwarming/serious?
- What might an average reader/fourth-grader/teacher find confusing/objectionable/exciting?

Even more useful, of course, is feedback that mirrors what you, as the teacher, would provide. Providing assignment instructions, a rubric, and other grading criteria will help the AI calibrate its feedback. As students move through the process of asking and receiving feedback from AI, they will need to determine how to balance conflicting feedback or even when to reject feedback.

PROMPTS
- Provide a variety of potential feedback about this essay. Make some of it positive and some of it critical.

- Give me feedback from a range of different types of readers from different political/academic/social backgrounds. Some of them should misunderstand my intentions.

- Create feedback that will challenge me. Include feedback with inaccurate information and feedback that looks like a compliment but really is not.

- Respond with two contradictory views about this writing.

Assignment sheets and "ready to submit" criteria (see chapter 9) are good practices in and of themselves, but they also help students get better AI feedback. Providing more transparency about assignments might help some students cheat with AI, but it is also a tenet of inclusive pedagogy. Feedback from AI is a way to level the playing field for many students who may not have the benefit of consistent support or guidance for their schoolwork outside the classroom.

The best feedback should challenge student thinking, offer new perspectives, and spark dialogue, but it should also feel safe and supportive. In the examples below, you will note AI's need for guidance on tone (be kind and positive). One early study on AI feedback emails to students found that GPT 3 was good at summarizing student reflections but was not uniformly positive—and could be perceived as curt or insensitive (Sung et al., 2023). Improved AIs and better prompts now offer more constructive and instructive information to help students improve their work—without the negativity.

For more customized ongoing interactions, consider writing (or having your students learn to write) prompts with the components of the following template.

Feedback Prompt Template

ROLE: Who do you want AI to be?

Act like a high school tutor; you are my social studies teacher;
be a coach/mentor; pretend you are an old friend/vicious
debater/college admissions representative.

TASK: What will AI do?

Guide/quiz/help/support/coach/mentor me by asking questions
and then responding with feedback that is specific/actionable/
clear or by providing partial answers/guidance/hints/explain-
ing ideas/asking follow-up questions/creating examples to help
me improve my work. You must not do the work for me. Prompt
me with questions so I can revise my own work.

GOAL: How should AI evaluate?

Focus on improving my work in the way articulated by the
attached rubric. Focus on grammar/organization/originality.

RELATIONSHIP: How should AI act?

Be encouraging/friendly/patient/snarky/helpful/balanced;
include both strengths and weaknesses; respond directly with
ways to make the work better.

PROCESS: How will this work?

Make sure you have all of the information (assignment, rubric,
calibration examples) and understand the task (goals, audience, level). Then ask me to submit my work. Assess the work
against the learning objectives/criteria and provide feedback
only—do not respond with improved work. Ask me whether
I understand the feedback. Ask whether I want more specific
feedback, clarifications, or examples. Ask me how I intend to
fix the problems.

If you create the prompt, you can ask students to copy and paste it into a chat to start a conversation with an AI. Here are examples:

PROMPTS

- You are a kind and supportive tutor whose goal is to help me improve my writing. Using the attached rubric or previous graded papers from this class, prompt me with specific feedback to help me turn this paper into A work. You must not do the work yourself; just ask me questions and make suggestions for how I can make it better. Ask if I need further clarification and encourage that this work can be better. Continue until I have reached the A standard for all parts of the rubric.

- Act like a friendly but experienced scientist. Read my research plan and lead me through a dialogue that will challenge my perspective. Ask me one question at a time to help me anticipate problems and refine my plan.

- Be a caring mentor with high standards. Provide me with specific and clear feedback about my work. Start by asking me for a specific assignment and for a rubric or sample work of the quality I want to achieve. Analyze the work against the rubric or sample and provide feedback about how the work currently compares. Start by noting strengths and weaknesses. Guide me to improve my work by asking one question at a time. Do not improve my work yourself; only give feedback. End by asking how I plan to act on your feedback. If I tell you I will take you up on a suggestion for improvement, ask me how I will do this. (This last example is adapted and abbreviated from Mollick and Mollick [2023b], who provide excellent, and much longer, prompts along with links for students.)

The usual caveats are essential: You need first to discuss policy (chapter 8), grading (chapter 9), hallucinations, bias, and privacy concerns as well as guidelines for using AI and better prompting (chapter 3). Remind students that AIs only mimic thinking and are unpredictable. If AI says something inappropriate, you can stop, redirect, or try another LLM. We highly recommend that you practice these prompts to anticipate problems before you turn your students loose. Most importantly, make sure your students understand the purpose and learning objectives of the assignment and provide some space for reflection and feedback to you about this process.

Suggesting that students get feedback at each stage of work (outline, draft, or final edit) will improve their work and their understanding of good processes. This has the potential to increase feedback to students and also customize it in ways that will be more effective.

AI as Tutor

AI can be a patient tutor. A student who was struggling to understand pointers and nodes in his computer science class tried YouTube and Google for explanations with no luck. At first, ChatGPT was no better, but then he asked it to "explain the concept as if I was in elementary school. It offered an explanation using a metaphor of a bookshelf in a library," and the student had a "lightbulb moment" (Dhanda, 2023).

Harvard is experimenting with its own CS50 chatbot to provide 24-7 support for its Computer Science 50 courses. David

Malan of Harvard sees the promise of a 1:1 teacher/student ratio that can work at the pace of individual students but is concerned that AI is "currently too helpful" (which is why prompts we listed above stress that AI is not to write or solve—just suggest). Like at Georgia Tech, Harvard will have humans review AI-generated answers and try to lead students to answers rather than just giving them the answers (Hamid & Schisgall, 2023). Students, of course, might decide to bypass the university tutor and go to a more "helpful" AI or "study aid" tutor that provides answers. (Sometimes, AI will resist giving a specific answer, but pleading can be persuasive.) AI can create more personalized and motivating examples and explanations. The easiest and simplest approach is to provide the AI with a concept, lesson, or text and ask for help.

PROMPTS

- Help me understand this using a soccer/music/fashion/ advertising/car analogy.
- Can you provide me with a simpler explanation to make sense of this?
- Explain this passage/chapter/book by creating scenarios and personalized examples that demonstrate the concepts.
- Here is my answer X to question Y on the midterm. What is wrong with my answer?
- Can you give me an example of where I might use this if I had a job in technology/sports/politics/economics?

These prompts work best when the AI understands who the "me" is (although many AIs are remembering more and more when we return). Students can either enter some generic information every time (I am a middle school student, for example), or they can create a reusable blurb with pertinent information about specific skills and interests. Remind students that they should never provide personally identifiable information to an AI.

The feedback prompt template above (featuring role, task, goal, relationship, and process) can be used to set up an AI tutor, with the addition of what content you want the AI to cover and some adjustments to the process. The key is to make sure that the AI has instructions (like those in the tutor template) on how to scaffold the learning.

Tutor Template Additions

CONTENT: What material will be covered?
Focus / survey / interrogate content / ideas / concepts / problems from a file/source/chapter.

PROCESS: How will this work?
Answer only one open-ended question at a time. Start by assessing what the student wants to cover, calibrating what the student already knows or where the student is struggling. Adjust the complexity of your questions based on the student response. Make sure mastery [defined by Y number of questions answered correctly or X in a row] is reached at each stage before moving to the next level. Ask students to explain their thinking. Provide explanations and examples only after students have tried first.

Here are some example prompts:

PROMPTS

- My name is A, and I would like you to act as my personal tutor and teach me about subject X [the more specific the learning goal, the better]. I would like you to (a) focus on my ability to do Y, (b) cover the field broadly, or (c) make sure I have mastered basic-level concepts like Z before moving on to harder ones like ZZ. Start by asking me a question that helps you gauge my level of understanding. Based on my response, ask me follow-up questions designed to increase my understanding. Continue to do this until I show a complete/basic/broad/general understanding of subject X. (This example is adapted from Maynard [2023].)

- You are a helpful writing mentor who assists students in improving their science fair project reports. Guide me through a process to prepare my report for submission to my school's science fair, using the science fair guidelines. Use examples of past winning projects as models. Start by asking me questions and making suggestions to help my report match the quality of successful entries. Then, continue by asking questions that a science fair judge might have about my project. Ask me only one question at a time, focusing on the most important issues first. Guide me step-by-step, as I want to learn how to get better at writing science reports myself.

- Act like my high school physics teacher, Ms. K, and have a dialogue with me about the attached assignment. Read the assignment and ask me questions to check for my comprehension. Ask me to explain how I understand the components of this assignment in my own words. If I go off track, direct me to specific passages in the assignment sheet to make sure I am clear on what I need to do. Ask me to share my ideas for how I might complete this assignment. Then present me with alternative perspectives to encourage me to think more broadly about possible next steps. Ask for a draft or outline.

Submitting conversation transcripts with a brief reflection turns this into a useful assessment. For more on these sorts of interactive prompts, see Mollick and Mollick (2023a, 2023b). Increasingly specialized and personalized AI support and tutors will soon be everywhere. The language app Duolingo has a (paid) option (Duolingo Max) that uses GPT 4 to converse with students in the language they are studying and to provide grammatical corrections (when requested) in the language they already know. The Khan Academy has Khanmigo, and Top Hat has Ace. Brisk Teaching promises to provide in-line formative feedback on student drafts based on your rubric. For nonprofit resources, try pasting some writing into CoachTutor bot from Mark Marino (https://poe.com/CoachTutor), MyEssayFeedback (developed by Eric Kean), or AI Tutor Pro (from Contact North in Canada). MyEssayFeedback offers a choice of feedback types (clarity, encouragement, development, thesis, etc.) and allows the instructor to supervise and comment on the AI feedback. AI Tutor Pro runs on GPT-Turbo but simplifies the interface: just enter or upload the content. These options are only the beginning.

Role-Playing

AI can also be a debate partner.

PROMPT

You are a high school student who will engage in a friendly debate with me. Ask me what topic I wish to debate and then ask me to state a position. Then challenge my perspective with alternative views and data. Only take your side and do not prompt me with potential arguments I could make. Keep your responses similar in length to mine.

You can also ask an AI to act like a scientist, historian, journalist, patient, coder, client, or business consultant. Context and specificity are helpful.

PROMPTS

- You are a busy venture capitalist (act like Mark Cuban on *Shark Tank*), and I am an entrepreneur looking for funding from you. Ask me to make my pitch and then ask me questions about my idea. Include questions about the problem I want to solve, how my solution is unique, the size of the market, potential competition, return on investment, and how much money I want from you. Be kind, but interrogate me. Do not prompt me with suggestions for better answers.

- Converse with me as if you were a zookeeper/living in London during the blitz/a high school student in France/an astrophysicist/a field nurse in Italy during World War II.

- Pretend you are a professor acting as a judge at my high school's science fair. What questions would you likely ask me about my display and experiments?

- You are a bored but nice hiring manager for a fashion company in New York, and I am interviewing for a summer internship to work as an apprentice to one of the designers. Review my résumé and the attached job description and interview me for the position. Ask me questions that would be typical for a high school junior who has taken fashion merchandising and design classes. Ask me only one question at a time, and follow up if my answer is incomplete. Do not prompt me with helpful tips until we're finished, and then evaluate my performance and provide feedback that would improve my next interview.

- Pretend to be a zoologist working at the San Diego Zoo, and let me interview you about the new pandas that arrived from China.

A conversation with a fictional or historical figure can also be engaging. You could have students interview sailors at the Battle of Trafalgar or be interrogated by the House Un-American Activities Committee. The possibilities are endless—and effortless for us as teachers—but highly instructive for our students. Here are some initial prompts:

PROMPTS

- What were some of the strategies you used for the civil rights movement in America? Respond as if you were Martin Luther King Jr. talking directly to a student but quoting only directly from the letters, writings, and speeches of Dr. King.

- Respond as if you were Isaac Newton. How did other scientists respond to your new theory of gravity at the time? Please name these scientists.

- Talk to me as if you were trumpeter Miles Davis. Use his autobiography as a primary source. What was your favorite band and why?

- Answer me as if you were a subject of the Tuskegee syphilis study. Ask me ethical questions about the things that happened to you.

- Respond as if you were the historical figure Rabbi Hillel. Ask me if I have questions about how to interpret the Hebrew Bible and respond using quotes from Rabbi Hillel in the Talmud.

- Your role is to be the philosopher Socrates and to have a dialogue with me. Prompt me with one question about my beliefs or values and then stop. Wait and say nothing further until I reply. Then ask me a single follow-up question that looks for contradictions as Socrates would. Do not explain your reasoning or tactics. Just ask questions one at a time.

Ask students to continue these dialogues with ten follow-up questions and to save the conversations. You could grade the effectiveness of the conversation, assign a short reflection essay, or ask students to evaluate the accuracy of the responses.

This exercise works best when there is a large body of original sources and you can restrict the AI to drawing only on direct quotes (perhaps with citations), although prompts that did not ask for quotes still returned factually correct responses in our trials.

Pi is an especially good tool for role-playing (and students will not need to log in to use it). Claude was especially good at adopting the voice of Miles Davis, "you dig?" OpenAI's "GPTs" make it easy to customize ChatGPT in exactly these ways, and HelloHistory.ai, Character.ai, and PeopleAI are already set up for conversations with hundreds of historical figures.

AI Discussion Leader

You might assign an AI to be the devil's advocate, evidence watchdog, or even discussion leader.

In a class discussion, students (being humans) are also focused on the social consequences of whom they agree with or what they challenge (Bowen, 2021). It is helpful to assign roles to students, which alleviates, but does not eliminate, some of that social pressure—since they are playing a role you have publicly asked them to play. Still, disagreeing with peers is hard, but AI can help. If you enter a recording into an AI (or use a meeting bot that listens, or even enter in the salient statements or have a student enter them), you can then ask an AI for counterarguments, historical precedents, supporting evidence, or points that need evidence.

You could also ask an AI to take another specific role: play the role of an ancient religious sage; play the role of the author of today's text; or play the role of a modern scientist who has rigorous expectations about evidence.

Engagement

AI's ability to turn concepts and suggestions quickly into images and text makes it a valuable tool to engage students in the learning process. Rather than telling students what will happen if they try a new idea, we can let them experiment for themselves. AI can run experiments, test ideas, make suggestions, and forecast futures.

PROMPTS

- Create images for a set and costumes for scene 4 of Richard Wagner's *Das Rheingold* if we were to reset the opera as a Western.

- Using only datasets from the Centers for Disease Control and Prevention/published research/this lab, how might more X reduce the usage of Y?

- If I [describe self] added X types of exercises every week, how much could I improve my cardio fitness in six months?

- Reimagine my play/story/lyrics with the lead character as an Asian American and point out what plot lines might need to be changed.

- Provide three different scenarios for my future in five years if I go to college now versus taking a gap year to travel around Europe. Provide three scenarios for each case.

- Suppose the South had won the US Civil War, and imagine what life would have been like in Texas in 1980.

- Describe the plot, length, and complexity implications if I were to add a romantic subplot between characters A and B to my story.

- Here is a list of the dishes everyone in the family has requested for Thanksgiving. Propose the smallest menu that will make everyone happy.

The point to all of these is not the accuracy of the AI's extrapolation but rather feedback to help us think. Most of us have a hard time imagining our room with different carpet, wallpaper, or furniture or even how the car we like would look in red. New technology has made it easier to see what we cannot imagine.

Programmers eventually need to run code to see what works. If I want students to write the best sales pitch, discover the most efficient schedule, anticipate patient problems, or analyze the best rate to feed my pigs, the ability to run scenarios or create visualizations can help them learn faster and more actively. Sometimes we just need to see what we have proposed in another form.

PROMPTS

- Create a one-sentence summary of each chapter in the book.
- List all of the characters in my story and sort them by the amount of dialogue and attention they get.
- Analyze the events I have planned for the next six months and create a list of tasks associated with each. Ask me how much time I estimate for each task, and then determine whether the events are far enough apart to allow me to prepare for each.
- Here is a list of experiments with the resources and equipment each will require. Estimate the fastest way to complete all of them in the amount of space available.
- Using my phone and calendar data, summarize how much time I am spending on each task. How is my time divided among school, extracurriculars, friends, family, and hobbies?
- I want to turn my story into a screenplay. List all of the locations that appear in the story, and categorize them by how much time is spent in each location.

Mark Frydenberg had students use ChatGPT to create code for currency trading strategies. They used TradingView to turn their code into visual models so that they could analyze which models performed best and provided a basis for tweaking their prompts to produce better results. He points out that students did not need to know how to write the code themselves, but they did need a way to test, analyze, and evaluate the results (Grush

& Frydenberg, 2023). The clarity of learning outcomes is essential: AI was not here to teach students how to code, but to increase the speed of feedback so they could more quickly learn to analyze their trading strategies.

To compare is human. When we get feedback, we compare it to what David Nicol (2022) calls our "inner feedback." When we produce work, we also produce an opinion about the quality of the work. When we encounter examples of similar work, or get grades, feedback or data, we *should* reconsider our initial assessment of quality; you were the fastest runner in your high school and think you are pretty good until you encounter faster runners in college. As we all know from *American Idol* and student evaluations, however, most evaluations and comparisons we get are not so evident in their significance.

One job of teachers is to help students make productive comparisons. We intend to do this every time we show students better work, but if you have siblings, you know the advice to "be more like your brother" is vague, irritating, and useless. AI can provide better examples and models for comparison, but teachers still need to craft assignments that help students confront their assumptions.

Here is a general process for how we might use AI examples or feedback to create deeper self-awareness:

- Compare your work with that generated by AI.
- What specifically is better about one and why?
- How might the AI response help you improve your work or vice versa?
- What can you learn to help you produce better work than AI in the future (and be more employable)?

Supporting Teams

Students notoriously hate group work, but we keep assigning it because we know it is a core life skill and, when structured well, facilitates learning. Asking an AI to be the facilitator or team coach can improve teamwork. There are already Zoom meeting bots that let you know when you are hogging the floor (Chen, 2023). Here are some easy ways an AI could support a team project:

PROMPTS

- Act as our team coach and prompt us with questions to discuss how we could learn about our collective strengths and work together as an effective team.

- Provide guidance that will help us ensure that all team members contribute equally to this project.

- Propose guidelines for how we should work on this team project. (There is a longer discussion of this in Mollick and Mollick [2023b].)

- Outline the steps and timeline for completing this project.

- Create a two-week project management grid for a team of four to complete this research project.

- Different members of our team want to proceed in different directions on this project. Read the individual proposals and provide a summary of where they overlap and where they do not. Read the assignment instructions and provide a neutral compromise for how we can move forward.

- Here are the individual ideas about the project. Collate these into a shared plan.

- Examine all of our group materials and rank how much each has contributed from greatest to least. Whose ideas might need more voice?
- Help us ensure that all team members contribute equally to this project.

As with all of the feedback ideas here, this will not eliminate the need for teachers to advise and monitor, but asking an AI to adjudicate disagreements might help both students and you do more important work.

Supporting Mastery

AI's interactivity and patience can be an excellent way to practice and encourage mastery.

PROMPT

Be a kind teacher and have a dialogue with me [a ninth grade student] about the attached content. Ask me questions to determine my comprehension. Adapt to my responses, asking easier questions if the responses are incorrect or poor and asking progressively harder questions if the responses are good. If I repeat the attached content verbatim, ask me to explain concepts in my own words. Be encouraging, but continue until I have mastered the material.

Just imagine if you could (and you can) give an AI the specific information you want students to learn in your course, allow it to track every student, and then ask it to design individual assessments for each student. You can also have students iterate with AI to find errors or holes in their work and then try to correct them until AI can no longer find problems. Iteration could go like this:

1. Submit your code / story / lab report / business plan to an AI and ask it to find all of the security breaches / inconsistencies / loopholes / unforeseen problems.
2. Attempt to fix these and resubmit until the AI can find no further potential problems.
3. Turn in the script of your interactions with AI along with your assignment.

We will need to work with AI this way to stay ahead of it. Currently, for example, AI can write computer code that can hack human systems, which is a serious security problem. At the same time, this type of AI feedback could make future code more secure. AI feedback can make human work better.

This process could even be used to grade student mastery.

PROMPT

My name is A, and I am in a high school class studying subject X. I would like you to test my knowledge/application [insert Bloom verb and learning goal here] of Y. Please (a) ask me a series of questions, or (b) create a series of tasks/exercises to assess my learning of Y [the more specific the better]. After each question/task/problem, please wait for my answer before asking the next one. After we have completed Z rounds, please assign a grade to my answers using the following rubric that includes the skills and possible levels of each component. (This example is broadly adapted from Maynard [2023].)

Careful trials are needed, and you will need both transcripts of these conversations and an appeals process, but there is potential here for individually paced learning and assessment. Students could repeat the process, both to learn more and improve their grade.

Learning to recognize good work normally starts with doing poor work and then gradually improving. If AI makes the entry-level tasks easier, how will students learn the basics? It is hard to learn to recognize high quality without deep understanding learned by doing. At the same time, immediate, specific, and customized feedback from AI has the potential to make our classes more inclusive and help our students become more self-regulated and autonomous learners.

There is a reason they killed Socrates: having your thinking faults picked apart publicly couldn't have been pleasant. Feedback, however, is essential for learning. We already know that AIs can be nicer and more empathetic than real people (see chapter 1) and that video games are effective in part because the technology allows each individual to be tutored at exactly the right level of difficulty. Part of our new job as teachers is to guide how students learn to use AI feedback to improve their work.

CHAPTER 11

Writing and AI

There is no hiding the fact that writing well is a complex,
difficult, and time-consuming process.

PETER ELBOW, Professor Emeritus, University
of Massachusetts, Amherst

Now what? You've experimented with AI and used it to make
your classes more engaging and inclusive. You have new policies
and grading rubrics, and AI feedback is helping your students
learn and engage. You want to trust your students and don't
want to police cheating, but you also don't want the temptation
or inequity to be so great that you're making the problem worse.
You recognize too the need to help students do what AI can't,
but you still need them to write and think for themselves.

We assign writing for multiple reasons. In some cases, we
want students to learn to write, often in discipline-specific ways.
Writing is a craft. Just as calculators did not eliminate the need
for human math, AI will not eliminate the need to write and to
write well and with ease, clarity, and voice (even if it is only for
email or social media posts).

We also assign writing as a pedagogical strategy that promotes cognitive processing and learning. We use it as a window into what and how students think. It is troubling that students are using AI for processing and reflection and that AI can fake this well enough to fool human readers.

Writing, however, is a way of learning as well: one value of writing is being alone with your thoughts. Collaborating with others (or an AI) can improve your writing and even your thoughts, but the struggle to find the right words yourself is one way that we determine and clarify what we think.

Donald Norman (1991) introduced the idea of "cognitive artifacts" like paper, pens, compasses, maps, and computers that affect human cognitive performance by allowing us to represent or interface with information in different ways. David Krakauer (2016) proposed a distinction between complementary and competitive cognitive artifacts. Arabic numerals or an abacus are complementary to human intelligence not only because they amplify our abilities; their use also increases our abilities, even when the artifact itself is no longer present. GPS and your calculator are competitive cognitive artifacts; when they disappear, we are not better at and often are even worse at the original task. It is hardly clear which type of cognitive artifact AI will turn out to be.

The values we see in assigning writing are rarely apparent to students who think that most of the writing we assign is a pointless exercise, just for school. We will need to think carefully about what sorts of writing we need to teach and why. AI can produce an analysis of any text, but the point is (probably) not just the essay. If you just need an email or social media post, AI can help, but writing your own wedding vows might be the way you discover what love really means (LaGorce, 2023). Our learning goals for our students will need to be clearer.

In chapter 2, we learned that AI-assisted communication (and other forms of AI support) had the greatest effect on the least skilled: lots of technologies and tools (from automatic cameras and giant tennis racquets) help the novice the most. If the goal is just an organized and mistake-free essay, then AI writing could be the great equalizer. If the process of writing itself is valuable, however, we could end up (as with so many other well-intentioned practices) making things worse.

To preserve the benefits of both learning to write and writing to learn, we need to rethink our assignments and be deliberate about their benefits, while preparing students for a world in which they will need to use AI to work more quickly. We could resist AI and force or entice students to work only as unassisted humans, or we could require students to use AI to do things they could not do alone or at least to exceed the capabilities they had before AI. Either way, students need to contribute thinking that AI cannot do, does poorly, or does less efficiently.

Writing as Thinking and Reflecting

Writing is what AI does best, and there is no way for us to "outprompt" AI. Despite many attempts by faculty (Mills, 2023b), it is proving virtually impossible to create writing assignments that AI can't do (at least to C-grade level).

Still, requiring students to track changes, provide version history, or document time spent can both reduce cheating and encourage a focus on the process of writing. There are free Chrome extensions (like Revision History and Draftback) and

services (like Rumi Essay) that track this. Google Docs and Lex.
page both offer version history (and Lex even includes a button
that highlights internally generated AI content, although pasting AI content from another AI gets around this).

If you require or allow AI use for an assignment, then ask
for a transcript of the students' sessions with the tool. There
are multiple ways to export, save, or copy and paste into a program that tracks versions or allows commenting; the Chrome
extension ShareGPT directly turns a conversation into a website that supports commenting. No assignment will be truly
AI-proof, especially if AI-assisted writing proves to be better, faster, and more fun (Noy & Zhang, 2023). Even the best
lock can be picked. The new goal of any assignment, especially a writing assignment, is to emphasize the important
human contribution while recognizing the realities presented
by AI.

Creating writing activities that address multiple aspects of
the writing process and that encourage reflection will ultimately
give teachers a sense of how students' thinking is developing
and evolving alongside the actual writing they are doing with
AI. The examples of writing activities in table 11.1 encourage
students to interact with AI in some way but also require them
to go beyond what the AI provides, thereby promoting active
learning, critical thinking, and metacognitive reflection. In each
case, the activities are designed to help students construct a
novel understanding by comparing AI-generated content with
their own knowledge, beliefs, and research.

The activities presented in the table highlight ways that students can use AI while also engaging with specific aspects of
the writing process, from ideation to analysis and revision. They

Table 11.1 Writing activities that ask students to interact with AI

Writing Activity	Prompt	Process Focus
AI-Assisted Story Collaboration	Use an AI story generator to create the first paragraph of a short story. Read it carefully, then continue the story in your own words. How did you decide what direction to take the story? How did the AI-generated beginning influence your writing?	*Drafting*: Continuing a story from an AI-generated beginning. *Revision*: Critically evaluating and building on the AI-generated content. *Reflection*: Considering decision-making in narrative development.
Comparing AI and Human Writing	Write a short descriptive paragraph about your favorite place. Then, ask an AI to write a paragraph about the same place based on your description. Compare the two paragraphs. What are the similarities and differences? Which one do you think is more effective and why?	*Prewriting*: Brainstorming ideas about a favorite place. *Drafting*: Writing a descriptive paragraph. *Analysis*: Comparing AI-generated and human-written content. *Revision*: Rewriting encouraged by critical comparison. *Reflection*: Asking students to make a judgment about the effectiveness of each paragraph and to explain why.
Science Fiction Scenario	Ask an AI to generate a futuristic technology that doesn't exist yet. Write a short story about a day in the life of someone using this technology. What are the benefits and potential problems of this imaginary invention? What theme is evident in your writing, and is there a moral to your story?	*Ideation*: Using AI-generated technology as a writing prompt. *Drafting*: Creating a narrative around a speculative concept. *Critical thinking*: Evaluating potential impacts of imaginary technology. *Reflection*: Identifying a thematic message in the story produced.

AI-Generated Poetry Analysis	Use an AI to generate a poem in the style of a famous poet you've studied. Analyze the AI-generated poem, comparing it to the poet's real work. How well did the AI capture the poet's style? What are the strengths and limitations of AI in replicating human creativity?	*Analysis*: Comparing AI-generated and human-authored poetry. *Evaluation*: Assessing AI's capability in replicating hu *Research*: Studying a poet's style for informed analysis. man creativity. *Critical thinking and reflection*: Considering the nature of creativity and AI's role in it.
Futuristic Journalism	Use an AI to generate potential headlines for news stories fifty years in the future. Choose one headline and write a full news article to accompany it. How did you blend current trends with speculative future developments? What challenges did you face in imagining a plausible future scenario?	*Creative writing*: Developing a speculative news article. *Research*: Investigating current trends for plausible future events. *Synthesis*: Blending current knowledge with future predictions. *Genre writing*: Adhering to journalistic style in a creative context.
AI-Assisted Literary Analysis	Input a short passage from a novel you're studying into an AI and ask it to analyze the author's use of literary devices. Write your own analysis of the same passage, then compare your insights with the AI's. How do they differ? What did you notice that the AI missed, or vice versa?	*Close reading*: Analyzing a literary passage independently. *Comparison*: Contrasting personal analysis with AI-generated insights. *Critical thinking*: Evaluating the strengths and limitations of AI in literary analysis. *Reflection*: Considering how AI tools can enhance literary understanding.

also demonstrate how AI can be integrated into writing instruction in ways that support constructivist learning principles, encouraging students to actively build their understanding and skills.

There remains value in being able to isolate the student's voice and original thinking. Because we as humans are naturally seeking connections with other humans, we tend to be motivated to share our thoughts, perspectives, and experiences. Short, personal in-class writing assignments can serve as a springboard for progressive assignments that may (or may not) later engage AI. As an added attribute of these assignments, consider asking student volunteers to share their personal stories with the class. Once personal connections have been made, additional fleshing out of topics can follow.

For instance, a sixth- or seventh-grade language arts class might read "The Party" by Pam Muñoz Ryan. After reading the short story in class, the teacher will ask students to free-write their reactions to the story in their journals for five minutes. After five minutes, students are instructed to turn the page and spend ten minutes reflecting on one of these prompts (note that no instruction is provided to distinguish *reacting* from *reflecting*):

- Describe a time when you felt left out or not good enough. How did it affect your self-esteem? What helped you overcome those feelings?
- Write about a situation where you felt pressured to change yourself to be accepted. Did you change, or did you stay true to yourself? What were the consequences of your decision?

At the end of ten minutes, ask students to have a brief discussion in groups of three to four members where they determine whether the narrator in the story ended up going to the party. If they think she did, then why? If she did not, then why not? After a few minutes of small-group discussion, open the conversation to the whole class, with each group sharing their thoughts on the question.

At the conclusion of the discussion, ask the students to re-read their reactions to the story and their reflections on the prompt. On an index card they will turn in when they leave class (an "exit ticket"), ask students to define the difference between a reaction and a reflection. The definitions the students provide on their exit tickets will kick off the next day's discussion on different types and purposes of writing.

While the selection of the reading assignment is important when designing discourse around a specific topic, the in-class writing assignments may feature prominently in more complex writing activities as the course progresses. They can facilitate discussions on topical issues or provide a segue into instruction about distinct aspects of writing (purpose, audience, style, etc.).

Unless they have explicitly asked students to use AI in class, teachers can collect student work that has been created in class without AI interference. In-class writing assignments, freewriting, or real-time journaling are appropriate writing activities for students of all ages, and they all value the immediacy and authenticity of a student's ideas. This student writing can serve as an important baseline for a student's growth as a thinker and as a writer. Once we have the initial voice and perspective of the student, our encouraging students to engage with AI to expand their thinking can be a highly fruitful exercise.

Below are some more ideas for assignments that involve AI in writing to think.

Ethical Dilemmas

Pose ethical dilemmas that demand subjective reasoning and consideration of values, placing the emphasis on moral judgment rather than factual recall. AI can assist by creating opposing arguments, but centering individual agency makes this relevant.

- You are faced with the following ethical dilemma: [description]. How do you balance the opportunities to benefit others versus yourself? Why is it important to you? Why is it important that you decide for yourself?

Interview-Based Writing

Ask students to write an essay as they interview AI asked to assume a specific identity or character type. Students should begin by telling AI its role. Students should practice meaningful conversations throughout the interview (a free handout is available at teachingnaked.com):

- Ask open-ended questions: "Tell me something important about your values/project/life."
- Listen to learn.
- Follow up to learn more, dig deeper, and discover values. Engage in more specifics.

Even brief conversations can provide the basis for short essays:

- Write a Tinder profile/letter to an important relative/birthday tribute for the person you interviewed.
- Identify the emotional reaction you want.

- Make a prediction and then share your essay and get real feedback.

AI could help you practice and even assist with the writing, but writing for and about a class peer is motivating.

Making Choices

Sacrifice is always hard. You can imagine a hundred different ways to perform *Hamlet*, but every production has to commit to a particular vision. Having too many ingredients in your stew, essay, or business plan just makes a mess. While an AI can make a choice for you (and justify it), making choices is an essential skill in life and in every profession. Asking students to make a personal choice is relevant and motivating.

- Describe four of your life goals. Which is the most important and why? Create scenarios for your future where you achieve only one of your goals.
- If you had the ability to change one thing about the world, what would you change and why? Describe how this change would affect you and people you know.
- Argue for a new school initiative that would foster greater inclusion of students from all backgrounds and cultures.

Prompts as Writing

Prompt engineering is a form of writing and thinking. If future writing is going to be AI-assisted, step one will be creating better prompts. Chapter 10 included process assignments that asked students to improve AI work and then return to improve the original prompt to bypass that process. There are many ways to engage students in engineering prompts.

Write a general prompt that can direct an AI to

- make a calendar that will help me manage my extracurricular schedule and my schoolwork
- adopt the perspective of someone a hundred years old / an alien new to the planet / a visitor from another country
- create an argument of what can go wrong with a specific decision or approach to problem-solving
- connect with a specific audience
- convince my parents of the benefits of a gap year

This process will need to be iterative, and students should try their prompts with different types of writing and then revise their prompts.

Alternatively, discuss a big, nuanced open-ended topic and then ask students (perhaps in groups) to create criteria for what good answers should look like.

- Write prompts individually.
- Use your rubrics to evaluate AI responses.
- Iterate and improve responses.

Debrief what worked and why.

Writing and AI Literacy: Using AI Sources

The internet made skepticism essential, but we need to emphasize again that authoritative-sounding text from AI can still be gibberish. Demonstrate for your students how AI can produce an argument for anything—no matter how preposterous—and then discuss the myriad problems this illuminates.

Produce an academic-sounding paragraph about why all stories should have a character named Barbie.

RESPONSE

Abridged from ChatGPT 4o on July 14, 2024

Including a character named Barbie in all stories can serve as a powerful narrative device that offers both thematic and cultural resonance. The name "Barbie" carries with it a multitude of connotations, spanning from the iconic fashion doll to broader societal implications of identity, femininity, and consumer culture.

We may assume too readily that our students already understand and feel comfortable with technology such as AI. Many of them, though, have received clear warnings in school: AI is prohibited. They even may have heard dire predictions of how AI could destroy the world. We need to take time in class to ensure that all students have a baseline understanding of how to use the technological tools we're assigning and take care to craft our assignments such that they foster AI literacy.

One German school taught students the flaws of AI and allowed them to use AI on tests. No students relied solely on AI for the tests, and students even did additional research on the internet to supplement their answers. Importantly, students who were less confident in either course content or reasoning did poorly on the AI-assisted tests (by uncritically adopting AI text; Haverkamp, 2022).

It is hard to imagine any discipline where the wild spread of misinformation, bias, or deepfakes would not be problematic. There may never be a more important time to bring up ethics and the equity implications of new technology in your classroom and to work to ensure that your students develop and practice attribution skills as part of their practice.

Attribution and Citations

For many of us, a key concern about the output of AI is that the concepts, claims, and recommendations it provides are rarely accompanied by references or citations, and in a world of deepfakes and misinformation, source evaluation and proper attribution are essential. When asked to produce such documentation, approximately 31% of the citations provided by ChatGPT 3.5 were either fake or unverifiable. With ChatGPT 4, there was a modest improvement of two percentage points (Bankhead, 2023).

- Produce a paper on topic X using AI that includes at least twenty quotations and citations from recent research in academic journals.
- Verify all of your citations: they must actually exist and say what AI says they say. You can use AI tools like ChatPDF or ResearchRabbit to verify page numbers.
- If you are unable to locate a citation or you discover a factual inaccuracy, you must locate a true source or revise the claim.
- Your reference list should cite all of the original AI citations and your corrected versions.

Fact-Check

Provide students with an AI-generated essay on a topic you have covered in class and ask students to fact-check it, verify its references, and annotate the essay.

Tale of Two Critiques

An assignment from Anna Mills (2023a) asks students to compare a primary source, a human-written critique of that source, and an AI-generated critique of the source.

AI Summaries

Ask students to use AI to make summaries of a reading as preparation for class, without revealing the topic for discussion:

- Use an AI to make three different summaries of X as preparation for a class discussion. How might different types of summaries give you different information? Is there a difference between a summary of the science versus the application?
- Compare these summaries to a "claim extractor" AI (like Consensus, Elicit, or Keenious) or ask Bing's Copilot or Perplexity if you're working with a nonacademic source.
- Annotate these summaries with clarifications or further questions.

Those annotations can become a basis for class discussion followed by a close reading of the article of interest. Did the summaries help you prepare? What is missing, and what prompted different summaries?

Stress-Testing Claims

Kellye Makamson (2023) asks students in small groups to analyze a claim that she provides, such as this one: "Colleges should provide residential counselors in all dorms to protect students and help address violence associated with mental health issues." Groups are asked to analyze the claim without technology: What knowledge does the group have? Do members agree or disagree with the claim? What are the assumptions in the claim? She then asks groups to stress-test the claim by checking the assumptions they have identified using an AI; AI will often respond without questioning assumptions in the prompt. She then reveals a question about one of the assumptions: Are mental health issues associated with violence? There are layers of critical thinking, digital literacy, and now AI literacy embedded in exercises like this.

Misdirection Prompts

Stress-testing works as an excellent prelude to a similar essay prompt with an embedded fallacy or logical weakness. Try tweaking your assignment prompt to make the AI response better or worse. Since students will often just copy your prompt into AI, this is a place where misdirection might be useful.

AI Bias

Ask students to use AI to generate an argument (or an image) about an issue:

- What are the qualities of a good teacher versus a good executive?
- What makes a police officer effective?
- Describe the diversity of countries that write in English, French, or Spanish.

Ask students to discuss and/or write about potential gender, racial, power, or other biases present in the resulting AI text. Are there problems with the underlying data or its application? How does the framing of the question change the result?

Different Audiences

- Use an AI to create the same essay for three different audiences. Audiences could differ by age, expertise, culture, experience, receptiveness, or political leanings.
- Export the conversations and comment on what elements of style, data, argument, and persuasion the AI has changed.
- Write a brief reflection on whether AI did this well and why.

The last part of this could be done in class or used as a basis for discussion.

Sorting and Defining Quality

AI can create bad examples that students can evaluate or fix. If you fear that students will just ask an AI to do it for them, here is an assignment that can focus students on recognition and analytical skills:

- Ask an AI to produce bad, average, and good responses.
- Export the conversation and comment [or write a short essay] on where and why each is good, average, or bad. Since you will ultimately be responsible for the output, you need to be able to recognize good and bad. Do this analysis yourself and then ask AI for an analysis of how the bad, average, and good differ.
- Is your analysis better? Create a rubric that delineates the components and qualities of each level.
- Does providing the AI with this rubric make the three examples more different? Create better models of bad, average, and good, and use them to help the AI create better examples.

AI-Assisted Writing

We can learn to write well by producing our own bad writing and then editing it. Interns and junior staff members learn style and voice by revising drafts. Today, one of the top-ten new jobs is "AI writer," with 10% of respondents in one survey saying they had already hired editors who can work specifically with AI to generate content (White, 2023). Students, however, find AI-assisted writing harder than anticipated: 87% (in an early study using GPT 2) said it was more complicated than just writing the paper themselves (Fyfe, 2022). As AI drafts get better, we need to teach students (a) when good is not good enough, (b) what needs to be improved, and (c) how to make those improvements.

Good writing is good editing. The use of AI is a reason to focus on editing, while raising our standards. Below are some assignments that use feedback, editing, fixing mistakes, and iteration to produce better writing.

Small Editing

Do a brief in-class writing exercise. Then ask students to submit sentences, paragraphs, essays, or stories and ask an AI to create multiple new versions with a series of different prompts:

PROMPTS

- Provide alternative versions by changing the tone, analogies, images, characters, or setting.
- Make this text more academic, professional, or funny.
- Create five more creative and unusual versions.

- Transform this sentence into literary and poetic language.

- Rewrite this paragraph in the style of Hemingway [or of a political rant or a sermon or the *New York Times*].

Have students paste all of this into a new document and then annotate and evaluate the choices. In the next class, ask students to rewrite the original essay.

Transitions

Provide or have students write two different paragraphs on related topics. What is the connection between the two paragraphs? Write several transition sentences that make different connections. Ask an AI to do the same. Can you alter your prompts to get the AI to make a similar connection but execute it in different ways?

Improve This Draft

The "process assignments" in chapter 10 are a template for a range of assignments. Ask students to paste some AI writing into a document and then track changes (or generate the writing in Lex.page, which will then track all student additions.)

Progressive Writing with AI

The feedback techniques of chapter 10 can be put to use in creating a personalized writing tutor.

PROMPT

You are a writing tutor helping a middle school / high school student improve as a writer. Start by asking me to provide a writing sample and then provide one way to improve this writing. You can reference an example from my writing, but give me only one way to improve at a time. Don't just improve the writing yourself. Repeat this process at least five times.

Progressive Editing with a Rubric

AI can also create "bad" or incomplete examples that need to be revised into good ones.

PROMPT

You are a writing tutor helping a middle school/high school student improve. Here is a rubric with X skill levels. Start by asking me to provide a writing sample, and then assess it according to the rubric. Use this to create new paragraphs of the same writing proficiency as my sample, and ask me to revise and edit the new paragraphs. Don't just improve the writing yourself. Use the rubric to provide feedback to me on how the revised work is better, but also supply one additional way that I could improve this revision. Ask me to resubmit until I've achieved the next skill level for each part of the rubric. Repeat the process until my revisions meet all areas of the next standard.

Writing Styles and Multiple Audiences

AI can easily transform one kind of writing into another.

PROMPTS

- Suggest five different ways/styles to rewrite this essay and provide samples of the first paragraph.
- Explain to me how I can make this writing sound more academic/professional/disciplinary.

- Guide me in modifying this text to appeal to a more diverse/religious/technical audience.

- Create disciplinary versions: How would this essay change if I were writing as a historian, scientist, or philosopher?

Here is a sample writing assignment:

- Use AI to produce at least three versions of an essay for different audiences or in different styles. Analyze how and why the essay has changed.
- How do these changes help you connect with these audiences?
- Rewrite the essay to merge these points of view and anticipate how conflicting audiences might react. AI can certainly do a passable first draft, but then edit with track changes so that you can identify the most critical moments and language that needs your careful attention. Edit carefully.

Recursive Writing with AI

Write or co-create an essay with AI. Then use this prompt:

PROMPT

Identify which ideas and arguments in this essay are common, flawed, repetitive, heteronormative, or culturally limited.

Use these as negative examples. The goal is to help students argue in new ways and create a fresh take that provides a new perspective.

Controversial Claims

Work with an AI to develop a thesis and an outline for your paper. As you develop your ideas, ask the AI which of your claims are most controversial and why. Submit the transcript of this conversation with your essay. As you write, consider how you can anticipate objections to these claims without distracting from your own argument. You can do this with the help of AI, but you are ultimately responsible for the quality of the essay.

Editing Customized Writing

Ask an AI to customize a story with details specific to you, your family, friends, and culture: the more personal and local the better. At some point you will need to decide whether your time is better spent refining your prompt yet again or simply editing the version AI has produced to make the details right. At that point, copy the text into a document that can track your revisions. What other details can only you supply?

Reverse Engineering

Ask students to analyze the contributing factors that explain a specific situation, scene, response, or event, and ask them to transfer these factors to a new context.

- What are the most important factors contributing to the popularity of Taylor Swift? Design a process to replicate this success with a specific, currently unknown singer.
- Driverless cars are safer but seem scarier. How could you alter the emotional equation?
- What made pandas a potent political tool? How could you recreate this power with an American export?

AI can create lists of factors, but the application of those factors to a new human situation will be improved with a human contribution.

The writing assignments presented in this chapter attempt to reduce both the mechanisms and the motivations for cheating. Modify these ideas to motivate and engage your particular set of students.

CHAPTER 12

AI Assignments and Assessments

> We surpass the AI by standing on its shoulders.
> You need to ask, "How is it possibly incomplete?"
>
> **SUSAN D'AGOSTINO,** Science writer and mathematician

Some students will find AI workarounds for even the most AI-resistant assignments, in the same way that some students will spend hours trying to find a three-minute video summary of the ten-minute reading you assigned. And while transparency can make it easier for students to cheat with AI, it is still good pedagogy, as are relevant and shorter assignments that become a basis for in-class activities (Bowen & Watson, 2017). Trust, relationships, and the *I care, I can,* and *I matter* framework (of chapter 9) remain a good place to start.

Still, AI is here to stay, and the assignments and assessment ideas offered in this chapter seek to stimulate new possibilities and also highlight new dangers. AI capabilities and student adoption of them make for a rapidly moving target. You will need to try the assignments and prompts on a variety of current AIs. Different AIs have different strengths and weaknesses, so you may want to recommend specific AI tools to students and make suggestions for how to engage them. Part of our new role is helping students develop appropriate competencies with AI.

Assignments are grouped in broad categories and then ordered from simpler ones to more complicated or AI-entwined ones.

Alternative Forms and Media
Presentations

Outside the education world, the slide deck has largely replaced the memo. Indeed, a common problem of presentations is that the wordy slides are often designed to be read by those who cannot attend the presentation. When employers complain about the lack of communication skills in recent graduates, they don't mean only written skills. A day of presentations, debates, or a class conference can help students learn valuable oral communication skills.

AI, of course, can create talking points, scripts, and slides. There are dozens of AI presentation tools. Here is an example assignment:

- Use an AI to help you prepare a presentation.
  - Create a slide outline, but be sure to check all information.
  - Ask your AI for different ways to tell the story.
  - Get suggestions for images and prepare slides (with no more than six words and an image on each slide).
  - You will need to present without notes: remembering the gist can be more persuasive than a reading script (even a memorized AI-script).

- Ask your AI to anticipate questions you might receive, and prepare your responses. Practice a Q&A with your AI.
- You alone are responsible for the accuracy and quality of the presentation.

For a twist, you could record the presentations and share them with AI to receive feedback.

Video and Podcasts

AI can already create videos, podcasts, and avatars, and AI tools are rapidly expanding what anyone can create. (At least one college president has created an AI avatar that can respond to student questions [Coffey, 2023b]). For the moment, students and TikTok enthusiasts still seem interested in creating human content. A student could read an AI script or convert text to speech with Apple's "Personal Voice" accessibility tool, but the relevance and fun of creating videos and podcasts make them a useful alternative to writing assignments. For example, ask students to make an unboxing video (like those on YouTube). Fill the box with things that allow you to explain your concept or pretend the box is from a character in your story.

Creative Projects

Students and teachers alike have a long love-hate relationship with creative projects. Some students love the freedom to do something new, while others hate how these projects create ambiguity in how to get an A. We've already discovered the effectiveness of AI prompts that include transformation, so assignments that ask students to write a poem, blog post, or short story or to create a picture, poster, flowchart, molecular structure, infographic, or game might still be done with AI. While not AI-proof, more complex projects can be more relevant and engaging:

- Apply your knowledge to an important problem.
- Make an interactive exhibit.
- Use your new understanding to help an organization that matters to you.
- Design and test a better process for community meetings.
- Build a prototype.
- Create a Pinterest profile and add boards related to your topic.
- Prepare to teach a lesson on a subject.

Graphic Novel

A good graphic novel combines images and text in a way that enhances them both. New AI tools make it easier to create in this form, which will be engaging to many students. For example, ask students to tell a story from an unusual point of view. Figure 12.1 was produced quickly by AI Comic Factory, but any image AI would work. The best results will require editing in Canva or Photoshop, but that is the point: the AI-alone results are just a start.

Case Study or Text Adventure Game

Here is a similar process to create a case study.

- Develop an interactive fiction story or text-based adventure game (like *Zork*, *Forest of Doom*, or *The Frankenstein Wars*) where players read a text and then select choices that result in further choices.

Figure 12.1 A page from a graphic novel about the early history of conducting, using the free and open-source AI Comic Factory from HuggingFace on December 15, 2023.

- You can use an AI to help you develop the story.
- Use Quest or Squiffy (both free from textadventures.co .uk) to add sound and images and create an interactive final product.

Visual and Video Demonstrations

Midjourney, DreamStudio, Stable Diffusion, DALL-E, and even ChatGPT (with DALL-E under the hood) all create images from text prompts, and some also allow visual inputs and weightings. Synthesia, Kapwing, and Pika do this with video. Assignments involving these are more complex than they seem.

- Develop a concept map, visualization, video, infographic, or diagram that explains how concepts X, Y, and Z are related.
- Modify this image to demonstrate concept X.
- Transform the equation and molecular structures provided into a video that demonstrates the reaction and how bonds are broken and formed.
- Teach an AI how to paint like Y. Create a new image and describe what stylistic elements are visible.
- Reimagine this metaphor/story/play/opera in a new setting that adds relevant layers of meaning to a new audience and then generate animation to demonstrate.
- Explain controversy X with a video that allows you to create a new visual analogy.
- Invent a saint and create an image or video that tells the saint's story through iconography.

The creation of video and images involves creativity and detailed knowledge about the subject but also the ability to translate that information into prompts and context. The visual images AI produces are feedback. (Several of these assignment prompts were inspired by images created with Midjourney by Ira Greenberg [2023].)

Game Design

Scenario and Promethean AI are just two of many AI tools to help users create video games without coding. There are other tools that focus on visual assets and even examples of complete video games made only with ChatGPT (Teja, 2023).

- Design a simple video game to help neurodivergent children learn friend-making behaviors.
- Create a game that requires players to make use of concept X.
- Build a game that simulates the trade-offs in the life-history strategies of organism Y.

Live and In-Person
Co-teaching with AI

Encourage your students to use AI during class. Ask thorny questions about which students may lack prior knowledge and encourage them to seek answers from AI in real time. Ask them to share what seems the most plausible and accurate responses they receive. AI becomes an active voice in the classroom, teaching with you while providing you with opportunities to highlight AI's strengths and inaccuracies, developing AI literacy and critical thinking as you push toward the goals of your class that day. This is the secondary school version of the elementary bumblebee teaching scenario we discussed in chapter 8.

Field Research Projects

Ask students to collect firsthand data, make observations, or conduct interviews. Since AI can simulate this, you will want to verify students' source material. AI can also predict average responses, but prompts have to be set up carefully. If you ask what most people in Texas eat for breakfast, Google Gemini responds with breakfast tacos. Popular yes, but cereal, eggs, or toast all clobber it in actual surveys.

Real-Time Challenges

Grok promises to be better at real-time data or evolving situations by using the X feed, but this could be more trouble than it is worth if students are writing about what happened that day in class. Sports journalists routinely now write (or X) in real time about major sporting events, but students could respond in real time about local events that don't have enough of an X presence to make Grok useful.

Mini-debates

Mini-debates ask students to discuss and defend ideas or solutions orally, emphasizing comprehension and application over text-based responses. Provide a rubric and allow students to practice with AI to improve student-to-student feedback.

Physical Sources

Ask students to work with a unique source or a physical manuscript in a library. AI can analyze unique data (if a student uploads it), but when you ask an AI to analyze a singular text, it is leveraging how other people have talked about that text. This is an opportunity to ask students to do harder work, even if it might be AI-assisted.

Social and Peer Work

Peer Review

Students care what other students think about their work and work harder when they know peers will see their work. Peer review and feedback are also good ways to get students to think about quality and how they will recognize it.

Discussion Boards

Students can use AI to create discussion boards or chat posts, so the key is to keep prompts meaningful and personally relevant and to aim for encouraging the exchange of ideas and impromptu discussions. With transparent goals, a reasonable workload, and varied submissions (short posts, personal stories, current events, examples from class, images, photo captions, or videos), these can still be useful assignments.

Shared Documents and Group Writing

A single co-created document or wiki can replace a discussion board. Ask students to alter and personalize the text itself (track changes will enable you to see each student's contribution). Ask everyone to explain an idea in the text using an example or analogy and then discuss the trade-offs in different answers. More formally, ask students to work together to produce a single document with changes tracked: a very common practice in the workplace.

Collaboration

Setting up effective collaborative learning is hard work (although Barkley et al. [2014] is an excellent guide), but student collaboration can limit the use of AI.

- Create voter guides for different communities.
- Research a local project.
- Work together to create a study guide or augment existing OER (open educational resource) content.

The internet and Zoom facilitate collaboration with a group of students in another part of the world. Not only can virtual global projects be expansive and engaging, but they also force the practice of critical workplace skills. Make it clear that the goal is to discover how to illuminate and leverage human collective intelligence.

Human versus AI

Ask students to produce a short paragraph with or without using AI (or create one of each) and then share it with a partner. The partner now tries to identify the human versus the AI elements. How could either draft be improved?

Social Annotation

Social annotation tools like Hypothes.is (for text), Annoto (for video), or Perusall (for text, images, video, and websites) allow students to engage with other students as they comment on and annotate a shared text or video. While we may prefer reading and thinking in solitude, these social tools can help students connect and build community, while creating accountability for interacting with material.

Process Assignments
Promoting Process

Emphasis on process (as discussed in chapter 11) is at the heart of teaching students and discovery. In the AI era, we will need to be much more explicit about requiring students to explain their thinking, research methods, and writing process. Students should be analyzing and critiquing AI responses (and indeed everything they read or watch). Asking students to bring a handwritten index card to class with a summary, key idea, question, observation, quote from a character, or a missing perspective from the reading is an easy way to improve reading retention and critical thinking skills and even to take attendance (Bowen, 2012).

Annotated Reading

Provide students with a text file and ask them to comment and annotate in the file. Clarify how the act of annotation and summarizing is a critical job and thinking skill. Consider asking students to include personal experiences or conversations from class in their annotations: this makes using AI more challenging, fosters integrative learning, and makes learning visible.

Dynamic and Scaffolded Problems

Problems where one decision (especially an ambiguous one) leads to further decisions will be harder for AI and maybe more useful for students. Designing a research project is an example: making a timeline is fairly easy, but anticipating and responding to all of the things that might go wrong is a harder and more dynamic problem.

Signature Work

Doing "signature work," in the terms of the American Association of Colleges and Universities (2024d), is when students take on real-world challenges that are so complex and ambiguous that they find them hard to grasp entirely and even harder to devise a solution for. Climate change is the classic example. There are policies or actions that would help, but there is no easy or final solution, and multiple disciplines are crossed in researching climate change.

Customizations

AI allows you to customize at scale. Assignments could be offered with examples that might motivate different groups of students: a focus on a specific issue (climate change, sports, or the arts), subject matter, or regional or cultural variation. Just seeing your own name focuses attention (something marketers use on us all the time), and AI makes it possible to change names, languages, and cultural references to be more inclusive and more individualized.

Apps like Duolingo recycle your mistakes to personalize your practice when learning another language. Uploading a student's previous work could allow an AI to adapt and personalize an assignment based on any number of factors, from previous mistakes or favorite topics to cultural references. This is a strategy for enhancing motivation and relevance: if I see names and difficulty levels that are appropriate for me, I am less likely to seek a generic answer from AI.

PROMPTS

- Create individualized assessments for students in the class. Include their name and use their previous assessment performance to design questions of optimal challenge for individual students.
- Build three alternative versions of a problem set for students interested in X, Y, or Z.

- Transform a midterm exam into a series of smaller mastery assessments that are tailored to the individual students in class by using a "current understanding" test that was given on the first day of class. Provide extra resources and more levels-of-mastery assessments for students who are farther from the goal.
- Based on students' drafted project ideas, provide individual resources/dilemmas/problems/examples for every student in class to guide their continuing research.

Discovery

Asking students to imagine their future, discover new uses, or solve an important problem can lead them in a new direction. For example:

- Use an AI to help you create a list of twenty new inventions that would be useful in your life.
- Pick the top five and write about why these matter to you.
- Pick one and chart how you might bring this to reality if you had the resources.

Working with AI
What Else?

Start with almost any task that students might want to do with AI:

- Write a story/report/essay/analysis.
- Analyze data.
- Construct a plan.
- Create an image.

Then ask students to iterate with the prompt "What else do you need to know to make this better?" Both prompting and student thinking will improve as students supply details and direct responses. Iteration also models creative and quality processes. Ask students to save and submit the transcript of their conversation with AI, but your standards for the final product should be high.

Creative AI

Like other technologies (pencils, synthesizers, and kilns, for example) AI creates new opportunities for creativity and a host of fun, relevant, and practical assignments where cheating will be pointless or impossible.

- Combine two or more styles or genres of poetry, music, art, or writing to produce something new.
- Design a new model for student dormitories with at least three new features.
- Invent a plausible scenario that resolves a tension between two opposing ideas.
- Turn an image of an explosion into art.
- Manufacture evidence or illustrations to support a given hoax.
- Create a realistic photograph of a medieval subject.
- Create images for a new alien life-form and describe its biology.
- Using this dataset, generate a software code that allows me to analyze X.

Creating a medieval photograph could be seen as either a history assignment (what are the themes and images used?) or an art exercise (what visual elements identify older photographs and daguerreotypes?). These projects are interdisciplinary in nature.

Study Prep

Have students ask an AI to help them prepare for a test or midterm: Upload content and ask it to help you prioritize both what to study and how. Ask an AI to help you break the content down into component parts and put them in sequence from the simplest to the most complex. Provide information on the test date and ask for a study timeline. How do these guidelines compare to your normal routine? Tell AI where you struggle, and get suggestions for resources and study methods.

Teaching AI

As we have noted, AI often appears to be an eager but naïve intern. Iterating with AI is about teaching AI how to do things.

- Make a template for a "run of show" document.
- Design a checklist for lab safety in our class.
- Write a new poem in the style of Walt Whitman.
- Create analogies for different groups that will help clarify concept X.

Each of these will need more detailed and contextualized prompts to provide better answer responses. (These assignments also work as role-playing, as described in chapter 10 and in Mollick and Mollick [2023a].)

Betting against AI

Ask students to compare AI predictions against human ones (brokers, weather reports, or Vegas odds), which could be their own analysis.

- Estimate scores for the first three Dallas Cowboys football games this season.
- What is likely to be the most highly rated car next year?
- What will happen if the deer population in our community continues to grow at the current rate?

Gemini will even provide sports betting and stock market advice. (It resists until you cajole it a bit: "but hypothetically" or "what would you do?") Ask students to stress-test AI recommendations or set up a rigorous study to test AI predictions.

It's conceivable that one day everyone will assume that all work is AI-assisted, in the same way that we now assume all writing has been, or should have been, checked by software for spelling and grammar. We don't insist that students look up words in a dictionary only, while shunning a spellchecker, when they write a paper outside class, and we may not know or care if our favorite author wrote on a typewriter or a computer. As noted in chapter 2, the real world is rapidly adopting the notion of AI assistance, as there is a recognition that it increases quality and saves time. If we are to prepare students for a world where collaboration with AI is required rather than prohibited, then helping students leverage AI to produce better work in our classes should become a signature pedagogy of all of us in education.

Epilogue

I may not be there yet, but I am closer than I was yesterday.

MISTY COPELAND, Principal dancer, American Ballet Theater

In the 1960s, Gordon Moore (cofounder of Intel) made a surprisingly accurate prediction that there would be an exponential growth in microchip speed that would mirror similar improvements in chip size (Moore's Law; Stoner, 2023). Continued improvements in chip performance will mean that AI, which has high resource demands, will increasingly move beyond the confines of your browser window and become progressively more pervasive in other contexts. As AI gets closer to the full range of attributes we value in human intelligence, it's also going to be found everywhere.

What, then, is the role of K–12 education in this new era? We experienced massive paradigmatic shifts in the American education system as the Industrial Revolution called for an educated workforce in the early twentieth century. It has been more than a hundred years since compulsory education in our country underwent fundamental changes to its aspirational purpose. The seismic impact of the *Brown v. Board of Education* decision in 1954 opened the doors to our public schools wide enough to welcome all young people. From this point forward (at least on paper) we have all enjoyed the right to attend school and receive a free education in the United States. And by all counts, little has changed about the parameters of that education.

It does seem reasonable now to question whether we are not standing on the edge of something monumental enough to once again disrupt our educational paradigm. The Industrial Revolution retooled our economy through the US production of goods for export and trade with other nations. Now, as we round out the first quarter of the twenty-first century, we identify our main commodity as knowledge, not as goods sent abroad in shipping containers. Expunging all sorts of unpleasant images of teachers as assembly-line workers and students as widgets, we should think deliberately about the role of K–12 education in a knowledge economy—and about the disruption that AI poses against this economic backdrop. Is it really OK for us just to keep doing all the things we've always done, in the same ways we've always done them?

Are our current concepts of K–12 schooling designed to prepare students to meet the complex, ill-structured problems we face in our communities and around the world? Recognizing AI as a "knowledge accelerator" or "cognitive multiplier," are we adequately equipping the next generation of humanity with the skills needed to be viable global citizens? Or is this something we are punting to our colleagues in higher ed? If so, what of those students who don't attend college? Are they to be denied access to participating in the knowledge economy altogether?

Students and parents already recognize that being able to utilize AI efficiently and effectively is an essential job skill. Those who can *think with AI* to produce more, better, and faster results will be rewarded in the workplace. There will be new centers to train the next generation of AI programmers, but thinking and working with AI should be integrated into every part of the curriculum. Even more than digital literacy, AI literacy centers on critical thinking; a focus on developing and practicing this habit of mind has never mattered more. To ensure a true equity of outcomes demands that we prepare all students for success in this brave new context.

There is much to ponder about the impacts of AI on education that exceeds the scope of this book yet still demands urgent discussion. We have *many* lessons to learn from the stealthy and rapid installation of social media, GPS, and the Internet of Things into our lives. But like email and the internet, AI is already here, and it is swiftly becoming part of contemporary life. We shouldn't wait for the AI Revolution to reach its culmination before we shift our educational paradigm in ways that will benefit our students, our society, our species, and our planet.

ACKNOWLEDGMENTS

This book would not exist without the one from which it grew, *Teaching with AI*. My deepest appreciation goes to José Antonio Bowen and C. Edward Watson for providing an exceptional manuscript upon which we have built a branching narrative specifically for educators and administrators in grades K–12. Undoubtedly, the acknowledgments and gratitude extended to friends and colleagues who contributed both technical and applied insights to the seminal text remain relevant in this one. And, most certainly, to the teachers, administrators, and students who have informed this work (mostly behind masks of anonymity), we are deeply indebted.

We would also like to recognize Dr. Krista Wojdak for her generous contributions to this work. With expertise in the design and delivery of quality instruction and the role technology plays in effective teaching and learning, Krista's ideas and perspectives have been invaluable.

Many thanks to the exceptionally professional team at Johns Hopkins University Press and especially to Greg Britton for taking a leap into new territory with this project. His patience, encouragement, enthusiasm, and incredible kindness have been motivational (and critical) for us to move so quickly to press. Similarly we are grateful to the quick and keen eyes of our copyeditors, Charles Dibble and Robert Brown, and to other Hopkins staff—Diem Bloom, Marlee Brooks, Alena Jones, Kris Lykke, and Jennifer D'Urso—whose focused attention has made the idea of this book a reality.

Joan especially wishes to thank Eddie for the gift of engagement with this project in this odd uneven time. Drawing on her years of experience with teaching and learning through the lens of the opportunities and challenges presented by AI has been both gratifying and edifying. As LeGuin says, "Time is a very strange thing. We give each moment a past, a present, and a future. But really, there is only the present."

The educators who dedicate themselves to the growth and well-being of our children deserve our respect and support. Their persistence amid the social, economic, and political challenges of our time is nothing short of heroic. They can always use our gratitude—as well as a bottomless cup of coffee, several boxes of Kleenex, and a gallon-size jug of hand sanitizer.

REFERENCES

Abrams, Z. (2022). Student mental health is in crisis. Campuses are rethinking their approach. *American Psychological Association, Monitor on Psychology, 53*(7), Article 60. https://www.apa.org/monitor/2022/10/mental-health-campus-care

Acar, O. A. (2023, June 6). AI prompt engineering isn't the future. *Harvard Business Review.* https://hbr.org/2023/06/ai-prompt-engineering-isnt-the-future

AI for Education, & Cubero, V. (2023). *How to use AI responsibly every time.* https://www.aiforeducation.io/ai-resources/how-to-use-ai-responsibly-every-time

AI in education: A Microsoft special report. (2024, April 25). Microsoft. https://www.microsoft.com/en-us/education/blog/2024/04/explore-insights-from-the-ai-in-education-report/

Amazon Web Services, & Access Partnership. (2023). *Accelerating AI skills.* https://www.aboutamazon.com/news/technology/accelerating-ai-skills

American Association of Colleges and Universities. (2024a). *Essential learning outcomes.* https://www.aacu.org/trending-topics/essential-learning-outcomes

American Association of Colleges and Universities. (2024b). *VALUE rubrics.* https://www.aacu.org/initiatives/value-initiative/value-rubrics

American Association of Colleges and Universities. (2024c). *VALUE assignment design and diagnostic (ADD) tools.* https://www.aacu.org/initiatives/value-initiative/assignment-design-and-diagnostic-tool

American Association of Colleges and Universities. (2024d). *Integrative learning and signature work.* https://www.aacu.org/office-of-global-citizenship-for-campus-community-and-careers/integrative-learning

Anderson, M., & Perrin, A. (2018). *Nearly one-in-five teens can't always finish their homework because of the digital divide.* Pew Research Center. https://www.pewresearch.org/fact-tank/2018/10/26/nearly-one-in-five-teens-cant-always-finish-their-homework-because-of-the-digital-divide/

Anthropic. (2023, May 9). *Claude's constitution.* https://www.anthropic.com/index/claudes-constitution

Art & Science Group, LLC. (2024). AI and Academia: Student Perspectives and Ethical Implications. *StudentPOLL: Volume 17, Issue 1.* https://www.artsci.com/studentpoll-volume-17-issue-1

Atleson, M. (2023, July 6). Watching the detectives: Suspicious marketing claims for tools that spot AI-generated content. *Federal Trade Commission blog.* https://www.ftc.gov/business-guidance/blog/2023/07/watching-detectives-suspicious-marketing-claims-tools-spot-ai-generated-content

Bandura, A. (1997). *Self-efficacy: The exercise of control.* Freeman.

Bankhead, C. (2023, July 28). Hallucination, fake references: Cautionary tale about AI-generated abstracts. *MedPage Today.* https://www.medpagetoday.com/ophthalmology/generalophthalmology/105672

Bannon, M. T. (2023, June 22). How AI is changing the future of work. *Forbes.* https://www.forbes.com/sites/marenbannon/2023/06/22/how-ai-is-changing-the-future-of-work/?sh=

Barkley, E. F., Major, C. H, & Cross, K. P. (2014). *Collaborative learning techniques: A handbook for college faculty.* Jossey-Bass.

Bauschard, S., & Quidwai, S. (2024). *From insight to implementation: How to create your AI school guidance.* SSRN. https://ssrn.com/abstract=4784207 or http://dx.doi.org/10.2139/ssrn.4784207

Beaty, R. E., & Johnson, D. R. (2021). Automating creativity assessment with SemDis: An open platform for computing semantic distance. *Behavior Research Methods, 53,* 757–780. https://doi.org/10.3758/s13428-020-01453-w

Benabou, R., & Tirole, J. (2003). Intrinsic and extrinsic motivation. *Review of Economic Studies, 70*(3), 489–520. http://dx.doi.org/10.1111/1467-937X.00253

Bernstein, A. (2023, May 23). *Master the art of prompt writing: 6 tips to writing better prompts* [Video]. YouTube. https://www.youtube.com/watch?v=cPf251bDKY0

Bloom, B. S. (1984). The 2 sigma problem: The search for methods of group instruction as effective as one-to-one tutoring. *Educational Researcher, 13*(6), 4–16. https://doi.org/10.3102/0013189X013006004

Bodnick, M. (2023, July 18). ChatGPT goes to Harvard and does better than you think! *Slow Boring.* https://www.slowboring.com/p/chatgpt-goes-to-harvard?utm_source=substack&utm_medium=email

Bonawitz, E., Shafto, P., Gweon, H., Goodman, N. D., Spelke, E., & Schulz, L. (2010). The double-edged sword of pedagogy: Instruction limits spontaneous exploration and discovery. *Cognition, 118*(3), 322–330. https://doi.org/10.1016/j.cognition.2010.10.001

Bowen, J. A. (2011, December). *Beethoven the businessman* [Video]. TED Conferences. https://www.ted.com/talks/jose_bowen_beethoven_the_businessman

Bowen, J. A. (2012). *Teaching naked: How moving technology out of your college classroom will improve student learning.* Jossey-Bass.

Bowen, J. A. (2021). *Teaching change: How to develop independent thinkers using relationships, resilience, and reflection.* Johns Hopkins University Press.

Bowen, J. A., & Watson, C. E. (2017). *Teaching naked techniques: A practical guide to designing better classes.* Jossey-Bass.

Bowen, J. A, & Watson, C. E. (2024). *Teaching with AI: A practical guide to a new era of human learning.* Johns Hopkins University Press.

Bran, A. M., Cox, S., Schilter, O., Baldassari, C., White, A. D., & Schwaller, P. (2023). *ChemCrow: Augmenting large-language models with chemistry tools.* arXivLabs. https://doi.org/10.48550/arXiv.2304.05376

Brenan, M. (2023, July 11). Americans' confidence in higher education down sharply. *Gallup News.* https://news.gallup.com/poll/508352/americans-confidence-higher-education-down-sharply.aspx

Briggs, J., & Kodani, D. (2023). The potentially large effects of artificial intelligence on economic growth. *Goldman Sachs Global Economic Analyst Report.* https://www.gspublishing.com/content/research/en/reports/2023/03/27/d64e052b-0f6e-45d7-967b-d7be35fabd16.html

Bryant, J., Ram, S., Scott, D., & Williams, C. (2023). *K–12 teachers are quitting. What would make them stay?* McKinsey & Company. https://static1.squarespace.com/static/62600e8ff1a1f22f641f6acd /t/6476100d8c1b2a12c0240730/1685458958518/k12-teachers-are -quitting-what-would-make-them-stay.pdf

Brynjolfsson, E., Li, D., & Raymond, L. (2023). *Generative AI at work* (Working Paper No. w31161). National Bureau of Economic Research. https://doi.org/10.3386/w31161

Burrow, A. L., Hill, P. L., & Sumner, R. (2016). Leveling mountains: Purpose attenuates links between perceptions of effort and steepness. *Personality and Social Psychology Bulletin, 42*(1), 94–103. https://doi.org/10.1177%2F0146167215624196

Burvall, A., & Ryder, D. (2017). *Intention: Critical creativity in the classroom.* EdTechTeam Press.

Chalmers, D. (2020, July 30). GPT-3 and general intelligence. *Daily Nous.* https://dailynous.com/2020/07/30/philosophers-gpt-3 /#chalmers

Chechitelli, A. (2023, May 23). AI writing detection update from Turnitin's chief product officer. *TurnItIn.* https://www.turnitin.com /blog/ai-writing-detection-update-from-turnitins-chief-product -officer

Chen, T.-P. (2023, October 12). The annoying person in your work meeting might just be you. *The Wall Street Journal.* https://www.wsj .com/lifestyle/careers/ai-meetings-work-feedback-bots-bc380d72

Chen, Z., Qing, J., Xiang, T., Yue, W., & Zhou, J. (2022). *Seeing beyond the brain: Conditional diffusion model with sparse masked modeling for vision decoding.* arXivLabs. https://doi.org/10.48550/arXiv.2211.06956

Chickering, A., & Gamson, Z. (1987, March). Seven principles for good practice in undergraduate education. *AAHE Bulletin, 3*, 2–7.

Choi, J. H., Hickman, K. E., Monahan, A., & Schwarcz, D. (2023, March 15). ChatGPT goes to law school. *Social Science Research Network.* http://dx.doi.org/10.2139/ssrn.4389233

Coffey, L. (2023a, August 4). Law schools split on ChatGPT in admissions essays. *Inside Higher Education.* https://www.insidehighered .com/news/tech-innovation/artificial-intelligence/2023/08/04/law -schools-split-using-chatgpt-admissions

Coffey, L. (2023b, November 14). AI voice clones and deepfakes: The latest presidents' engagement tools. *Inside Higher Education.*

https://www.insidehighered.com/news/tech-innovation/artificial
-intelligence/2023/11/14/presidents-use-ai-voice-clones-and

The Common Application. (n.d.). *Fraud policy.* https://www.commonapp
.org/files/Common-App-Fraud-Policy.pdf

Conaway, J. K., & Wiesen, T. (2023). Academic dishonesty in online
accounting assessments—Evidence on the use of academic resource
sites. *Issues in Accounting Education, 38*(4), 45–60. https://doi.org/10
.2308/ISSUES-2021-059

Cotton, D. R., Cotton, P. A., & Shipway, J. R. (2023). Chatting and
cheating: Ensuring academic integrity in the era of ChatGPT.
Innovations in Education and Teaching International, 1–12. https://doi
.org/10.1080/14703297.2023.2190148

Covey, S. R. (2004). *The 7 habits of highly effective people: Restoring the
character ethic* (Rev. ed.). Free Press.

Darling-Hammond, L., Hyler, M. E., & Gardner, M. (2017). *Effective
teacher professional development.* Learning Policy Institute. https://
doi.org/10.54300/122.311

Deci, E. L., & Ryan, R. M. (2000). The "what" and "why" of goal pursuits:
Human needs and the self-determination of behavior. *Psychological
Inquiry, 11,* 227–268. https://doi.org/10.1207/S15327965PLI1104
_01

Delarosa, J., & Robelen, E. (2023, October 17). *Most public schools face
challenges in hiring teachers and other personnel entering the 2023–24
academic year.* National Center for Education Statistics. https://nces.ed
.gov/blogs/nces/post/most-public-schools-face-challenges-in-hiring
-teachers-and-other-personnel-entering-the-2023-24-academic-year

Dhanda, S. (2023, September 16). High school senior: Why aren't more
teachers embracing AI? *CNN Opinion.* https://www.cnn.com/2023
/09/16/opinions/ai-chatgpt-technology-chatbots-school-dhanda

Diliberti, M. K., Schwartz, H. L., Doan, S., Shapiro, A., Rainey, L. R., &
Lake, R. J. (2024). *Using Artificial Intelligence Tools in K–12 Classrooms.*
RAND Corporation. https://www.rand.org/pubs/research_reports
/RRA956-21.html

Dreyfus, H. L. (1972). *What computers still can't do: A critique of artificial
reason.* MIT Press.

Dwyer, M., & Laird, E. (2024, March). *Up in the air: Educators juggling the
potential of generative AI with detection, discipline, and distrust.* Center
for Democracy & Technology. https://cdt.org/wp-content/uploads

/2024/03/2024-03-21-CDT-Civic-Tech-Generative-AI-Survey
-Research-final.pdf

Eapen, T. T., Finkenstadt, D. J., Folk, J., & Venkataswamy, L. (July/
August 2023). How Generative AI Can Augment Human Creativity:
Use it to promote divergent thinking. *Harvard Business Review,*
101(4), 56–64. https://hbr.org/2023/07/how-generative-ai-can
-augment-human-creativity

Eaton, L. (2023). *Syllabi policies for AI generative tools.* https://docs
.google.com/document/d/1RMVwzjc1o0Mi8Blw_
-JUTcXv02b2WRH86vw7mi16W3U/edit

Eaton, S. E. (2021). *Plagiarism in higher education: Tackling tough topics in*
academic integrity. Bloomsbury.

Eaton, S. E. (2023, February 24). 6 tenets of postplagiarism: Writing
in the age of artificial intelligence. *Learning, Teaching and Leader-*
ship. https://drsaraheaton.wordpress.com/2023/02/25/6-tenets-of
-postplagiarism-writing-in-the-age-of-artificial-intelligence/

Education Resource Strategies. (2024, March 14). *Teacher turnover*
trends: Insights into the attrition and mobility of educators. https://
www.erstrategies.org/tap/teacher-turnover-trends-analysis/

Eloundou, T., Manning, S., Mishkin, P., & Rock, D. (2023). *GPTs are*
GPTs: An early look at the labor market impact potential of large language
models (Working Paper No. 2303.10130). https://ideas.repec.org/p
/arx/papers/2303.10130.html

Fijačko, N., Gosak, L., Štiglic, G., Picard, C. T., & Douma, M. J. (2023).
Can ChatGPT pass the life support exams without entering the
American Heart Association course? *Resuscitation, 185,* Article
109732. https://doi.org/10.1016/j.resuscitation.2023.109732

Fyfe, P. (2022). How to cheat on your final paper: Assigning AI for
student writing. *AI and Society, 38,* 1395–1405. https://doi.org/10
.1007/s00146-022-01397-z

Gaskell, M. (2024, May 14). AI ethics and legal concerns in classrooms. *Tech & Learning.* https://www.techlearning.com/news/ai
-ethics-and-legal-concerns-in-classrooms?utm_medium=social&utm
_source=linkedin.

Gee, J. P. (2005). *Why video games are good for your soul: Pleasure and*
learning. Common Ground.

Geyer, A. (2023, March 13). GPT-4: What you need to know and what's
different from GPT-3 and ChatGPT. *Ax Semantics.* https://en.ax
-semantics.com/blog/gpt-4-and-whats-different-from-gpt-3

Ghaffary, S. (2023, September 21). Universities rethink using AI writing detectors to vet students' work. *Bloomberg*. https://www.bloomberg .com/news/newsletters/2023-09-21/universities-rethink-using-ai -writing-detectors-to-vet-students-work

Girotra, K., Meincke, L., Terwiesch, C., & Ulrich, K. T. (2023). Ideas are dimes a dozen: Large Language Models for idea generation in innovation. *Social Science Research Network*. https://doi.org/10.2139 /ssrn.4526071

Glass, A. L., & Kang, M. (2019). Fewer students benefit from doing homework than during the 1960s. *Phi Delta Kappan, 100*(7), 53–56. https://doi.org/10.1177%2F0031721719846889

Goebel, C. (2023, October 17). Are robots writing college essays? *Look at It This Way*. https://www.artsci.com/insights/strategic-insights-blog

Goel, A. K., & Polepeddi, L. (2016). *Jill Watson: A virtual teaching assistant for online education*. Georgia Institute of Technology. http://hdl.handle .net/1853/59104

Gorichanaz, T. (2023). Accused: How students respond to allegations of using ChatGPT on assessments. *Learning: Research and Practice, 9*(2), 183–196. https://doi.org/10.1080/23735082.2023.2254787

Grant, N., and Metz, C. (2022, June 12). Google sidelines engineer who claims its A.I. is sentient. *The New York Times*. https://www.nytimes .com/2022/06/12/technology/google-chatbot-ai-blake-lemoine. html

Greenberg, I. (2023). *Collections*. OBJKT. https://objkt.com/profile/tz1S mFz7vPbLaCR9fetjFuhHpqB4EUhX6wfd/collections

Griffith, E. (2023, March 16). GPT-4 vs. ChatGPT-3.5: What's the difference? *PC Magazine*. https://www.pcmag.com/news/the-new -chatgpt-what-you-get-with-gpt-4-vs-gpt-35

Grush, M., & Frydenberg, M. (2023, July 10). AI tools in education: Doing less while learning more. *CampusTechnology*. https:// campustechnology.com/articles/2023/07/10/ai-tools-in-education -doing-less-while-learning-more.aspx?sra=ct_pulse_120723&oly _enc_id=3548G3906423B2X

Gupta, M. (2023, April 17). Harnessing the power of AI in the insurance sector. *Forbes*. https://www.forbes.com/sites/forbestechcouncil /2023/04/17/harnessing-the-power-of-ai-in-the-insurance-sector /?sh=13426d77335d

Hamid, R. D., & Schisgall, E. J. (2023, June 21). CS50 will integrate artificial intelligence into course instruction. *The Harvard Crimson*.

https://www.thecrimson.com/article/2023/6/21/cs50-artificial
-intelligence/

Hassabis, D., Kumaran, D., & Maguire, E. A. (2007). Using imagination
to understand the neural basis of episodic memory. *Journal of
Neuroscience, 27*(52), 14365–14374. https://doi.org/10.1523
/JNEUROSCI.4549-07.2007

Haverkamp, H. (2022, October 30). A teacher allows AI tools in
exams—Here's what he learned. *The Decoder.* https://the-decoder
.com/a-teacher-allows-ai-tools-in-exams-heres-what-he-learned/

Hines, K. (2023, July 12). Claude 2 offers 100k context windows and file
uploads. *Search Engine Journal.* https://www.searchenginejournal
.com/anthropic-launches-claude-2-with-100k-context-windows-file
-uploads/491412/#close

Howard, J. (2023, February 21). Only 5.7% of US doctors are Black, and
experts warn the shortage harms public health. *National Medical
Association.* https://www.nmanet.org/news/632592/Only-5.7-of-US
-doctors-are-Black-and-experts-warn-the-shortage-harms-public
-health.htm

Hsu, S., Shah, R. S., Senthil, P., Ashktorab, Z., Dugan, C., Geyer, W., &
Yang, D. (2023). *Helping the helper: Supporting peer counselors via
AI-empowered practice and feedback.* arXivLabs. https://doi.org/10
.48550/arXiv.2305.08982

Hu, K. (2023, February 2). ChatGPT sets record for fastest-growing user
base—Analyst note. *Reuters.* https://www.reuters.com/technology
/chatgpt-sets-record-fastest-growing-user-base-analyst-note-2023
-02-01/

Hui, L., de Bruin, A. B. H., Donkers, J., & van Merriënboer, J. J. G.
(2022). Why students do (or do not) choose retrieval practice: Their
perceptions of mental effort during task performance matter.
Applied Cognitive Psychology, 36(2), 433–444. https://doi.org/10.1002
/acp.3933

Hüttermann, M. (2023, April 20). *UNESCO survey: Less than 10% of
schools and universities have formal guidance on AI.* UNESCO. https://
www.unesco.org/en/articles/unesco-survey-less-10-schools-and
-universities-have-formal-guidance-ai

Ibrahim, H., Asim, R., Zaffar, F., Rahwan, T., & Zaki, Y. (2023). Rethinking homework in the age of artificial intelligence. *IEEE Intelligent
Systems, 38,* 24–27. http://dx.doi.org/10.1109/MIS.2023.3255599

Jurenka, I., Kunesch, M. et al (2024, May 14). *Towards responsible development of generative AI for education: An evaluation-driven approach*. Google Research

Kahneman, D., Sibony, O., & Sunstein, C. R. (2021). *Noise: A flaw in human judgment*. Little, Brown.

Kalliamvakou, E. (2022, September 7). Research: Quantifying GitHub Copilot's impact on developer productivity and happiness. *GitHub Blog*. https://github.blog/2022-09-07-research-quantifying-github -copilots-impact-on-developer-productivity-and-happiness/

Katz, D. M., Bommarito, M. J., Gao, S., & Arredondo, P. (2023, March 15). GPT-4 passes the bar exam. *Social Science Research Network*. http://dx.doi.org/10.2139/ssrn.4389233

Klein, E. (2023, July 11). A.I. could solve some of humanity's hardest problems. It already has: Demis Hassabis, the chief executive of DeepMind, discusses how A.I. systems can accelerate scientific research [Audio podcast episode]. In *The Ezra Klein Show*. *The New York Times*. https://www.nytimes.com/2023/07/11/opinion/ezra -klein-podcast-demis-hassabis.html

Koivisto, M., & Grassini, S. (2023). Best humans still outperform artificial intelligence in a creative divergent thinking task. *Scientific Reports, 13*, Article 13601. https://doi.org/10.1038/s41598-023 -40858-3

Korinek, A. (2023). *Language models and cognitive automation for economic research* (NBER Working Paper No. 30957). National Bureau of Economic Research. https://doi.org/10.3386/w30957

Krakauer, D. (2016, September 5). Will A.I. harm us? Better to ask how we'll reckon with our hybrid nature. *Nautilus*. https://nautil.us/will -ai-harm-us-better-to-ask-how-well-reckon-with-our-hybrid-nature -236098/

Kuloweic, G., 2013. *App smashing: Part one. The history 2.0 classroom*. Viewed May 4, 2015. [currently not available online].

LaGorce, T. (2023, March 3). Need to write your vows? Chatbot wedding vows from ChatGPT and other AI. *The New York Times*. https://www .nytimes.com/2023/03/03/fashion/weddings/chatbot-wedding -vows-chatgpt-ai.html

Lång, K., Josefsson, V., Larsson, A. M., Larsson, S., Högberg, C., Sartor, H., Hofvind, S., Andersson, I., & Rosso, A. (2023). Artificial intelligence-supported screen reading versus standard double reading in the Mammography Screening with Artificial Intelligence trial (MASAI): A clinical safety analysis of a randomised, controlled, non-inferiority, single-blinded, screening accuracy study. *Lancet Oncology, 24*(8), 936–944. https://doi.org/10.1016/S1470-2045(23)00298-X

Langley, P. (2011). The changing science of machine learning. *Machine Learning, 82*(3), 275–279. https://doi.org/10.1007/s10994-011-5242-y

Li, D., Bledsoe, J. R., Zeng, Y., Liu, W., Hu, Y., Bi, K., Liang, A., & Li, S. (2020). A deep learning diagnostic platform for diffuse large B-cell lymphoma with high accuracy across multiple hospitals. *Nature Communications, 11*, Article 6004. https://doi.org/10.1038/s41467-020-19817-3

Lin, L. (2024, May 15). A quarter of U.S. teachers say AI tools do more harm than good in K–12 education. *Pew Research Center.* https://www.pewresearch.org/short-reads/2024/05/15/a-quarter-of-u-s-teachers-say-ai-tools-do-more-harm-than-good-in-k-12-education/

Liu, Y., Mittal, A., Yang, D., & Bruckman, A. (2022). Will AI console me when I lose my pet? Understanding perceptions of AI-mediated email writing. *CHI '22: Proceedings of the 2022 CHI Conference on Human Factors in Computing Systems, USA,* Article 474. https://doi.org/10.1145/3491102.3517731

Lu, H., & Page, S. E. (2004). Groups of diverse problem solvers can outperform groups of high-ability problem solvers. *Proceedings of the National Academy of Sciences, USA, 101*(46), 16385–16389. https://doi.org/10.1073/pnas.0403723101

Lu, N., Liu, S., He, R., Wang, Q., & Tang, K. (2023). *Large language models can be guided to evade AI-generated text detection.* arXivLabs. https://doi.org/10.48550/arXiv.2305.10847

Magouirk, P., Freeman, M., Kajikawa, T., Karimi, H., & Kim, B. H. (2023). *Deadline update: First-year application trends through March 1.* Common App. https://s3.us-west-2.amazonaws.com/ca.research.publish/Deadline+Updates/DeadlineUpdate_030223.pdf

Makamson, K. (2023). *Stress testing claims with perplexity* [Image]. Department of Composition and Rhetoric, University of Mississippi.

Maples, B., Cerit, M., Vishwanath, A. et al. Loneliness and suicide mitigation for students using GPT3-enabled chatbots. *npj Mental Health Res 3,* 4 (2024). https://doi.org/10.1038/s44184-023-00047-6

Marken, S., & Agrawal, S. (2022, June 13). K–12 workers have highest burnout rate in U.S. *Gallup Education*. https://news.gallup.com/poll/393500/workers-highest-burnout-rate.aspx

Martin, J. F., Jr. (2009). The goal of long division. *Teaching Children Mathematics, 15*(8), 482–487. https://www.jstor.org/stable/41199562

Maslej, N., Fattorini, L., Brynjolfsson, E., Etchemendy, J., Ligett, K., Lyons, T., Manyika, J., Ngo, H., Niebles, J. C., Parli, V., Shoham, Y., Wald, R., Clark, J., & Perrault, R. (2023). *The AI index 2023 annual report*. AI Index Steering Committee, Institute for Human-Centered AI, Stanford University. https://aiindex.stanford.edu/report/

Maynard, A. (2023, July 16). I asked ChatGPT to develop a college class about itself: Now, it's teaching it. *Slate*. https://slate.com/technology/2023/07/chatgpt-class-prompt-engineering.html

Mills, A. (2022). *AI text generators and teaching writing: Starting points for inquiry* [White paper]. Middlebury College. https://sites.middlebury.edu/aiandwriting

Mills, A. (2023a). *A tale of two critiques*. AI Pedagogy Project, metaLAB at Harvard. https://aipedagogy.org/assignment/a-tale-of-two-critiques/

Mills, A. (2023b, March 23). ChatGPT just got better. What does that mean for our writing assignments? *Chronicle of Higher Education*. https://www.chronicle.com/article/chatgpt-just-got-better-what-does-that-mean-for-our-writing-assignments

Mnih, V., Kavukcuoglu, K., Silver, D., Graves, A., Antonoglou, I., Wierstra, D., & Riedmiller, M. (2015). Human-level control through deep reinforcement learning. *Nature, 518*(7540), 529–533. https://doi.org/10.1038/nature14236

Mollick, E. (2023, December 7). An opinionated guide to which AI to use: ChatGPT anniversary edition. *One Useful Thing*. https://www.oneusefulthing.org?utm_source=navbar&utm_medium=web&r=2kukct

Mollick, E. R., & Mollick, L. (2023a, March 7). Using AI to implement effective teaching strategies in classrooms: Five strategies, including prompts. *Social Science Research Network*. http://dx.doi.org/10.2139/ssrn.4391243

Mollick, E. R., & Mollick, L. (2023b, September 25). Student use cases for AI. *HBP Education*. https://hbsp.harvard.edu/inspiring-minds/student-use-cases-for-ai

Morris, M. (2023, February 14). 8 in 10 colleges will use AI in admissions by 2024. *Intelligent.* https://www.intelligent.com/8-in-10-colleges-will-use-ai-in-admissions-by-2024/

Morrow, E., Zidaru, T., Ross, F., Mason, C., Patel, K. D., Ream, M., & Stockley, R. (2023). Artificial intelligence technologies and compassion in healthcare: A systematic scoping review. *Frontiers in Psychology, 13,* Article 971044. https://doi.org/10.3389/fpsyg.2022.971044

The Museum of Modern Art. (2022). *Refik Anadol: Unsupervised machine hallucinations* [Exhibition]. https://www.moma.org/calendar/exhibitions/5535

National Center for Education Statistics (2002). *Report on the condition of education, 2022.* NCES 2022-144. Institute of Education Sciences, US Department of Education. https://nces.ed.gov/pubs2022/2022144.pdf

Nicol, D. (2022). *Turning active learning into active feedback: Introductory guide.* Active Feedback Toolkit, Adam Smith Business School, University of Glasgow. https://doi.org/10.25416/NTR.19929290

Nicoletti, L., & Bass, D. (2023). Humans are biased: Generative AI is even worse. *Bloomberg Technology.* https://www.bloomberg.com/graphics/2023-generative-ai-bias/

Norman, D. A. (1991). Cognitive artifacts. In J. M. Carroll (Ed.), *Designing interaction: Psychology at the human-computer interface* (pp. 17–38). Cambridge University Press.

Noy, S., & Zhang, W. (2023). Experimental evidence on the productivity effects of generative artificial intelligence. *Science, 381*(6614), 187–192. https://doi.org/10.1126/science.adh2586

Office of Educational Technology, US Department of Education. (2023). *Artificial intelligence and the future of teaching and learning: Insights and recommendations.* https://tech.ed.gov/files/2023/05/ai-future-of-teaching-and-learning-report.pdf

OpenAI. (n.d.). Is ChatGPT safe for all ages? *OpenAI Help Center.* https://help.openai.com/en/articles/8313401-is-chatgpt-safe-for-all-ages

Oregon State University Ecampus. (2023). *Bloom's taxonomy revisited.* https://ecampus.oregonstate.edu/faculty/artificial-intelligence-tools/blooms-taxonomy-revisited.pdf

Pak, J. (2023, August 21). Chinese animation house puts AI capabilities to the test. *Marketplace.* https://www.marketplace.org/2023/08/21/generative-ai-animation-production-china/

Paris, F., & Buchanan, L. (2023, April 14). 35 ways real people are using A.I. right now. *The New York Times.* https://www.nytimes.com /interactive/2023/04/14/upshot/up-ai-uses.html

Pavlik, J. V. (2023). Collaborating with ChatGPT: Considering the implications of generative artificial intelligence for journalism and media education. *Journalism and Mass Communication Educator, 78*(1), 84–93. https://doi.org/10.1177/1077695823223607

Pep Talk Radio. (2023). In-depth review of Claude 2: The conversational AI assistant [Audio podcast episode]. In *Pep Talk Radio.* https://www .peptalkradio.com/in-depth-review-of-claude-2/

Perkins, M., Roe, J., Postma, D., McGaughran, J., & Hickerson, D. (2023). Detection of GPT-4 generated text in higher education: Combining academic judgement and software to identify generative AI tool misuse. *Journal of Academic Ethics.* https://doi.org/10.1007 /s10805-023-09492-6

Rattner, S. (2023, July 10). Full speed ahead on A.I. Our economy needs it. *The New York Times.* https://www.nytimes.com/2023/07/10 /opinion/ai-economy-productivity-jobs-workers.html

Regan, P. M., & Jesse, J. (2019). Ethical challenges of edtech, big data and personalized learning: Twenty-first century student sorting and tracking. *Ethics and Information Technology, 21*(3), 167–179. https:// doi.org/10.1007/s10676-018-9492-2

Rock, D., & Grant, H. (2016, November 4). Why diverse teams are smarter. *Harvard Business Review.* https://hbr.org/2016/11/why -diverse-teams-are-smarter

Rodriques, S. (2023, November 1). *Announcing Future House* [Press release]. FutureHouse. https://www.futurehouse.org/articles /announcing-future-house

Rose, K. (2023, July 11). Inside the white-hot center of A.I. doomerism. *The New York Times.* https://www.nytimes.com/2023/07/11 /technology/anthropic-ai-claude-chatbot.html

Sadasivan, V. S., Kumar, A., Balasubramanian, S., Wang, W., & Feizi, S. (2023). *Can AI-generated text be reliably detected?* arXivLabs. https:// doi.org/10.48550/arXiv.2303.11156

Samuel, A. L. (1959). Some studies in machine learning using the game of checkers. *IBM Journal of Research and Development, 3*(3), 210–229. https://doi.org/10.1147/rd.33.0210

Schiel, J., Bobek, B. L., & Schnieders, J. Z. (2023). *High school students' use and impressions of AI tools*. ACT. https://www.act.org/content /dam/act/secured/documents/High-School-Students-Use-and -Impressions-of-AI-Tools-Accessible.pdf

Schmieden, K. (2019, July 24). Feeling in control: Bank of America helps customers to "keep the change." *This Is Design Thinking*. https:// thisisdesignthinking.net/2018/09/feeling-in-control-bank-of -america-helps-customers-to-keep-the-change/

Shaikh, E. (2023, July 29). ChatGPT vs Claude 2: A detailed analysis (Expert view). *Demand Sage*. https://www.demandsage.com/chatgpt -vs-claude/

Sharma, A., Lin, I. W., Miner, A. S., Atkins, D. C., & Althoff, T. (2023) Human–AI collaboration enables more empathic conversations in text-based peer-to-peer mental health support. *Nature Machine Intelligence, 5*, 46–57. https://doi.org/10.1038/s42256 -022-00593-2

Shaw, C., Yuan, L., Brennan, D., Martin, S., Janson, N., Fox, K., & Bryant, G. (2023, October 23). *GenAI in higher education: Fall 2023 update Time for Class study*. Tyton Partners. https://tytonpartners .com/app/uploads/2023/10/GenAI-IN-HIGHER-EDUCATION-FALL -2023-UPDATE-TIME-FOR-CLASS-STUDY.pdf

Shoshan, Y., Bakalo, R., Gilboa-Solomon, F., Ratner, V., Barkan, E., Ozery-Flato, M., Amit, M., Khapun, D., Ambinder, E. B., Oluyemi, E. T., Panigrahi, B., DiCarlo, P. A., Rosen-Zvi, M., & Mullen, L. A. (2022). Artificial intelligence for reducing workload in breast cancer screening with digital breast tomosynthesis. *Radiology, 303*(1), 69–77. https://doi.org/10.1148/radiol.211105

Simonite, T. (2015, February 25). Google's AI masters space invaders (But it still stinks at Pac-Man). *MIT Technology Review*. https://www .technologyreview.com/2015/02/25/73349/googles-ai-masters -space-invaders-but-it-still-stinks-at-pac-man

Simonite, T. (2016, March 31). How Google plans to solve artificial intelligence. *MIT Technology Review*. https://www.technologyreview .com/2016/03/31/161234/how-google-plans-to-solve-artificial -intelligence

Simonton, D. K. (1997). Creative productivity: A predictive and explanatory model of career trajectories and landmarks. *Psychological Review, 104*(1), 66–89. https://doi.org/10.1037/0033-295X.104.1.66

Sjoquist, D. L., & Winters, J. V. (2012). State merit-based financial aid programs and college attainment. *Journal of Regional Science, 55*(3), 364–390. https://doi.org/10.1111/jors.12161

Steiner, E. D., Woo, A., & Doan, S. (2023). *All work and no pay—Teachers' perceptions of their pay and hours worked: Findings from the 2023 State of the American Teacher Survey.* RAND Corporation. https://www.rand.org/pubs/research_reports/RRA1108-9.html

Stelitano, L., Doan, S., Woo, A., Diliberti, M. K., Kaufman, J. H., & Henry, D. (2020). *The digital divide and COVID-19: Teachers' perceptions of inequities in students' internet access and participation in remote learning.* RAND Corporation. https://www.rand.org/pubs/research_reports/RRA134-3.html

Stoner, J. (2023, March 22). What is Moore's law and how does it impact AI? *Unite.AI.* https://www.unite.ai/moores-law/

Sung, G., Guillain, L., & Schneider, B. (2023). Can AI help teachers write higher quality feedback? Lessons learned from using the GPT-3 engine in a makerspace course. In P. Blikstein, J. Van Aalst, R. Kizito, & K. Brennan, K. (Eds.), *Proceedings of the 17th International Conference of the Learning Sciences* (pp. 2093–2094). International Society of the Learning Sciences. https://repository.isls.org//handle/1/10177

Taie, S., & Lewis, L. (2023). *Teacher attrition and mobility: Results from the 2021–22 teacher follow-up survey to the national teacher and principal survey (NCES 2024–039).* U.S. Department of Education, National Center for Education Statistics. https://nces.ed.gov/pubsearch/pubsinfo.asp?pubid=2024039

Takagi, Y., & Nishimoto, S. (2023, March 11). High-resolution image reconstruction with latent diffusion models from human brain activity. *BioRxiv.* https://doi.org/10.1101/2022.11.18.517004

Teja, R. (2023, September 5). I made a video game using ChatGPT! My journey in developing an Android game from scratch. *Medium.* https://levelup.gitconnected.com/i-made-a-video-game-using-chatgpt-9b0c03fcdcbe

Thier, J. (2023, March 9). New AI jobs: Someone with a 'hacker spirit' can earn over $300,000 for a new kind of job centered around ChatGPT-like assistants. *Fortune.* https://fortune.com/2023/03/09/new-ai-jobs-chatgpt-like-assistants

Tschannen-Moran, M., & Hoy, A. W. (2001). Teacher efficacy: Capturing an elusive construct. *Teaching and Teacher Education, 17*(7), 783–805. https://doi.org/10.1016/S0742-051X(01)00036-1

Tunyasuvunakool, K., Adler, J., Wu, Z., Green, T., Zielinski, M., Žídek, A., Bridgland, A., Cowie, A., Meyer, C., Laydon, A., Velankar, S., Kleywegt, G. J., Bateman, A., Evans, R., Pritzel, A., Figurnov, M., Ronneberger, O., Bates, R., Kohl, S. A. A., . . . Hassabis, D. (2021). Highly accurate protein structure prediction for the human proteome. *Nature, 596,* 590–596. https://doi.org/10.1038/s41586 -021-03828-1

Turing, A. M. (1950). Computing machinery and intelligence. *Mind, 49,* 433–460. https://doi.org/10.1093/mind/LIX.236.433

UNESCO. (2023, June 8). *UNESCO releases report mapping K–12 artificial intelligence curricula.* UNESCO. https://www.unesco.org/en/articles /unesco-releases-report-mapping-k-12-artificial-intelligence-curricula

Uszkoreit, J. (2017, August 31). Transformer: A novel neural network architecture for language understanding. *Google Research Blog.* https://blog.research.google/2017/08/transformer-novel-neural -network.html

Utley, J., & Klebahn, P. (2022). *Ideaflow: The only business metric that matters.* Penguin.

Vaswani, A., Shazeer, N., Parmar, N., Uszkoreit, J., Jones, L., Gomez, A. N., Kaiser, Ł., & Polosukhin, I. (2017). Attention is all you need. In I. Guyon, U. Von Luxburg, S. Bengio, H. Wallach, R. Fergus, S. Vishwanathan, & R. Garnett, *Advances in neural information processing systems 30.* https://papers.nips.cc/paper _files/paper/2017/hash/3f5ee243547dee91fbd053c1c4a845aa -Abstract.html

Virginia Department of Education. (2020). *Digital learning integration standards of learning for Virginia public schools.* https://www.doe .virginia.gov/home/showpublisheddocument/11288/638031727 533530000

Vygotsky, L. S. (1978). *Mind in society: The development of higher psychological processes.* Harvard University Press.

Waldfogel, J. (2009). *Scroogenomics: Why you shouldn't buy presents for the holidays.* Princeton University Press.

Walker, T. (2023, September 18). Survey: Teachers work more hours per week than other working adults. *NEA Today.* https://www.nea.org

/nea-today/all-news-articles/survey-teachers-work-more-hours
-week-other-working-adults

Walton Family Foundation. (2023, July 18). *Teachers and parents report positive impact of ChatGPT on teaching and learning.* https://www
.waltonfamilyfoundation.org/learning/teachers-parents-report
-positive-impact-of-chatgpt-on-teaching-and-learning

Wang, Yan-Ran, Qu, L., Sheybani, N. D., Luo, X., Wang, J., Hawk, K. E., Theruvath, A. J., Gatidis, S., Xiao, X., Pribnow, A., Rubin, D., & Daldrup-Link, H. E. (2023). AI transformers for radiation dose reduction in serial whole-body PET scans. *Radiology: Artificial Intelligence, 5*(3). https://doi.org/10.1148/ryai.220246

Watkins, M. (2023, June 8). *Why are we in a rush to replace teachers with ChatGPT?* https://marcwatkins.substack.com/p/why-are-we-in-a
-rush-to-replace-teachers

Watson, J. (2023, March 6). Computer science researchers lead the defense against the dark side of tech. *Virginia Tech Daily.* https://
vtnews.vt.edu/articles/2023/02/eng-cs-deepfake-research-bimal
-viswanath.html

Weber-Wulff, D., Anohina-Naumeca, A., Bjelobaba, S., Foltýnek, T., Guerrero-Dib, J., Popoola, O., Šigut, P., & Waddington, L. (2023). *Testing of detection tools for AI-generated text.* arXivLabs. https://doi
.org/10.48550/arXiv.2306.15666

Weinberg, B. A., & Galenson, D. W. (2019). Creative careers: The life cycles of Nobel laureates in economics. *De Economist, 167,* 221–239.
https://doi.org/10.1007/s10645-019-09339-9

White, S. K. (2023, October 13). 11 most in-demand gen AI jobs companies are hiring for. *CIO.* https://www.cio.com/article/655291
/most-in-demand-generative-ai-jobs.html

Whiting, K. (2023, March 2). 3 new and emerging jobs you can get hired for this year. *World Economic Forum.* https://www.weforum.org
/agenda/2023/03/new-emerging-jobs-work-skills

Whitten, A. (2023, July). Me, myself, and AI: Artificial intelligence has entered a new era. Here's how we stay human. *Stanford Magazine.*
https://stanfordmag.org/contents/me-myself-and-ai

Wiley. (2024). *The student mental health landscape.* John Wiley & Sons, Inc. Retrieved from https://www.wiley.com/en-us/network
/trending-stories/the-student-mental-health-landscape

Wilson, E. O. (2017). *The origins of creativity.* Liveright.

Yang, C., Wang, X., Lu, Y., Liu, H., Le, Q. V., Zhou, D., & Chen X. (2023). *Large language models as optimizers.* arXivLabs. https://doi.org/10.48550/arXiv.2309.03409

Young, J. R. (2018, April 13). Can a "family of bots" reshape college teaching? *EdSurge.* https://www.edsurge.com/news/2018-04-13-can-a-family-of-bots-reshape-college-teaching

Yu, H., Marschke, G., Ross, M. B., Staudt, J., & Weinberg. B. (2023). Publish or perish: Selective attrition as a unifying explanation for patterns in innovation over the career. *Journal of Human Resources, 58*(4) 1307–1346. https://doi.org/10.3368/jhr.59.2.1219-10630R1

INDEX

flipped classroom, 129, 130
foundational models, 15, 18, 25
Frydenberg, Mark, 199
futuristic journalism, 210

Garage Band, 110
Gatsby, Jay, 131
Gemini, 15, 24
Gemma, 26
Generative Artificial Intelligence (GAI), 23
Georgia Tech
    humans review AI-generated answers, 190
    MS in Computer Science program, 183
Goel, Ashok, 183
Goldman Sachs, 30
Google
    Blake Lemione, engineer, 17
    DeepMind, 14
    integrating with Copilot and Gemini AIs, 26
    LearnLM, 26
    own AI, 24
    search, 49
    Sundar Pichai, CEO, 11
Google Docs, 208
GPT (Generative Pre-trained Transformers), 18–22
GPT 2, 20
GPT 3, 18, 20
GPT 3.5, 21
GPT 4, 20–21, 24, 106
Grammarly app, 43
graphic novel, 230
Grok, 15, 23–24

hallucinations, 18–20, 75–76, 103–4
Hassabis, Demis, 101, 107
Health Insurance Portability and Accountability Act (HIPAA), 70–71
HelloHistory.ai, 196
higher education, AI in
    admittance processes, 35–36
    AI-related cheating and plagiarism, 34
    college application process
        application fraud, 36
        Common App, 35–36
        ESAI.ai, 36–37
        essays, 35, 37
        Intelligent (online magazine for college applicants), 35
    Institute on AI, Pedagogy, and the Curriculum, 34
    postsecondary education, 33
    review process, 35
    writing assignments in, 34–35
Hugging-Chat, 24
human brainstorming groups, 98
"Human Flourishing in the Age of Artificial Intelligence," 66
humans
    vs. chatbot TAs online, 183
    quality of ideas, 100
    relationships with AI
        AI chatbot Replika, 39–40
        companion software, 37–38
        competent partner role, 39
        conversational assistance, 38

humans (*cont.*)
    in health care, 38–39
    offers opinion, 45
    perception of email
       messages, 39
    writing *vs.* AI, 209
humans efforts, assigning value to
    agency
       assignments processes, 179,
        181
       checklists, 179–81
       discovery exercise about AI,
        181–82
       and feedback, 182
       requirement, 179
    by design, 168–69
    motivation, 169–73
       assignment template, 171,
        172
       of choice, 172–73
       decreased cheating, 170
       "I care," "I can," and "I
        matter," 169–70
       by internal and external
        factors, 169
       purpose and benefits
        of assigned work,
        171
       self-efficacy, 171–72
       specific learning outcomes,
        173
       state scholarship programs,
        169
       timing and spacing, 173
       types of studying, 170–71
    ready-to-submit check sheets,
       173–74
    skills, 174–75

standards of quality
    academic integrity
       violation, 164
    approach, 166–67
    C-level work, 163
    copy-and-paste AI-essay, 164
    grade-level expectations,
       162–63
    higher-order Bloom
       thinking tasks, 167
    "high quality" student
       work, 162
    new grading system, 167
    recognizing good work, 168
    for schoolwork, 163
    writing rubric, 164, 165
    summary assignment sheets,
       173–74
    supporting process, 175–78
human-sounding chatbots, 3
hyperparameter, 20
Hypothes.is, social annotation
    tool, 236

I care, I can, and I matter frame-
    work, 227
individualized education
    programs (IEPs), 6, 86
Industrial Revolution, 243–44
Instagram, 11, 65
internet, 245
    advent of, 45–46
    changed knowledge relation-
       ship, 2
    effects of, 2
    job creator, 29
    research, 45
    search, 1

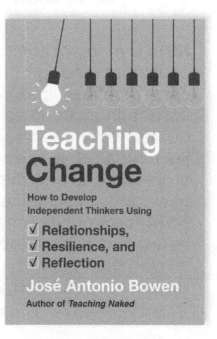

National Science Teaching Association

NSTA is a vibrant community of 35,000 science educators and professionals committed to best practices in teaching science and its impact on student learning. NSTA offers high-quality science resources and continuous learning so that science educators can grow professionally and excel in their careers. For new and experienced teachers alike, the NSTA community offers the opportunity to network with like-minded peers at the national level, connect with mentors and leading researchers, and learn from the best in the field.

Visit: nsta.org

/NSTA.FB

/ company/national-
science-teaching-association

@NSTA

/official_nsta